Yes You Can
Dr. Barb's Recipe for Lifelong Intimacy

by Dr. Barb DePree

Informative blog posts from
MiddlesexMD®

ISBN 978-1-312-30286-0

Yes You Can: Dr. Barb's Recipe for Lifelong Intimacy

While our information has been carefully prepared, it is not intended to be used for self diagnosis or treatment and does not substitute for medical diagnosis and treatment. Before starting or stopping any treatment or acting upon any information contained in the site, consult with your own physician or health care provider.

© 2014 DePree Women's Wellness, LLC, Douglas, Michigan

Book design by Kolk Creative

With deep appreciation to the many women who've taught me over the 25 years I've been practicing medicine, and to the MiddlesexMD team, especially Julie, Lois, Kris, and Kate.

Yes You Can: Dr. Barb's Recipe for Lifelong Intimacy

TABLE OF CONTENTS

INTRODUCTION

1. FACE THE CHANGE 1

    Keep on Learning
    Let's Get Aroused
    Why We Love Rosemary
    Our Secret Recipe for Sex after Menopause
    Boomer Sex: We've Got a Lot to Learn
    Not Tonight, Dear: Why We "Don't Feel Like It"
    An Open Letter: How to Really Turn Me on
    An Open Letter: Down and Dirty
    You Never Know: Staying Ready for Sex
    Questions... and Answers

        *Perimenopause * Mental Fog and PMS*
        ** Lack of Interest * Desire*

2. INTENTION AND INTIMACY 28

    What Subtracts More than it adds?
    What Is a Happy Marriage?
    Romance Awareness Month: Seize the Day
    A Little Conversation about Mindfulness
    Make Time Stand Still: The Body Scan
    Sex: Deciding to Just Do It
    Warming Up to Foreplay
    Satisfaction: It Works Both Ways
    Is Sleeping Apart the End of Sex?
    Your House Is Not Your Own?
    Movies to Turn You On
    Hitting the Sexual "Reset" Button
    Prayer and Sex: Not Such Strange Bedfellows
    Grow Toward Forgiveness
    Sex Therapy: Not So Scary After All
    Questions... and Answers

        *Intimacy * Unfulfilling Sex * Erotic Videos*
        * Emotionally Remote Partner

3. PLAYING IT SAFE 58

    So Over Contraception?

STIs: Not Just Your Daughter's (or Granddaughter's) Concern
When Was the Last Time You Used a Condom?
The Virus that Doesn't Go Away
Questions... and Answers
> HPV Risk * Re-Infection * Abnormal Pap * Birth Control Options

4. GETTING COMFORTABLE 69
We Shall Overcome: Dryness
Moist Is Good
Vaginal Health Begins with Bugs
"Nothing to Be Done about Pain?" Not So.
Pain during Sex? Escape the Cycle
The Ultimate Couple's Project: Pain-Free Sex
Vaginal Patency for Single Women
Keeping Things Open
Questions... and Answers
> Pain and Hypersensitivity * Lack of Desire * Lubricants and Moisturizers * Moisturizer Application * Estrogen Cream * "Hitting a Wall"

5. THAT LOVING FEELING 85
Female Anatomy 101
The Big O (And We Don't Mean Oprah)
Her First Vibrator
Dr. Krychman's "Meet Your Vibrator"
Vibrators for Two
The G-spot: Defined but Not Demystified
When an Orgasm Is Not an Orgasm
Warming Oils and Lubricants: Hot Topicals
What Do Breasts Do for Us?
Seeing Red
Need Help with Kegels?
> Patience, Patience!

Questions... and Answers
> Elusive Orgasm * Stress * Vibrator Success * Shrinking Tissues * Kegel Exercise Balls * Pelvic Floor Damage

6. THE HORMONE CONUNDRUM 114
One Test Where Grades Don't Count

Make Your Own Love Potion
E Is for Estrogen
Estrogen Where It's Needed
Testosterone: Not for Men Only
Beyond the Headlines: Evaluating HRT Risks
Bioidentical Hormones: Flap? Or No Flap?
Questions... and Answers
> *Moisturizer and Hormones * High Libido * Ring or Cream * HRT and Cancer*

7. HEALTH REALITIES AND HOPE 130
I Will Overcome
Sex and Arthritis: A New Kind of Reach
Sex and Depression
Sex and Back Pain: A Work-around Primer
Sex after Heart Disease: Good for the Body, Good for the Heart
Breathing Problems (COPD) and Sex: Take My Breath Away
Sex and Cancer
After Cancer: Take Care of Your Vagina
Missing Orgasm: Is It Me or My SSRI?
Prostate Cancer's Impact on You
Questions... and Answers
> *MS and Orgasm * Implications of Diabetes * Vaginectomy * Tamoxifen*

8. COMPONENTS OF GREAT SEX 154
Intro
Being present
Connection
Deep sexual and erotic intimacy
Extraordinary communication
Exploration, risk-taking
Authenticity
Vulnerability
Transcendence

RESOURCES 164
Resolve to Speak Up!
Having "The Talk" with Your Doctor
For More Information

INTRODUCTION

My interest in sex at midlife—and beyond—began when I partnered with my hometown hospital to evaluate local women's health services, looking for any gaps where additional services were needed. It became clear that our community needed and could support a health care practice devoted to the special needs and care of women who were past their childbearing years—these special needs were largely ignored by existing providers.

I decided to transform my practice from general obstetrics and gynecology into something more specific. I studied and became certified by the North American Menopause Society (NAMS) as a menopause care provider, and while welcoming patients into my practice, used their questionnaire—a thorough document that makes it easy for new patients to give me a comprehensive view of their symptoms and health histories.

On that eight-page-long form there are just a few questions for women to answer about their current and past sexual experiences:

» Do you have concerns about your sex life?

» Do you have a loss of interest in sexual activities (libido, desire)?

» Do you have a loss of arousal (tingling in the genitals or breasts, vaginal moisture, warmth)?

» Do you have a loss of response (weaker or absent orgasm)?

» Do you have any pain with intercourse (vaginal penetration)? If yes, how long ago did the pain start? Please describe the pain: Pain with penetration? Pain inside? Feels dry?

Well, I was amazed by the responses from my new patients.

Sixty percent of my patients have experienced a loss of interest in sexual activities, 45 percent have a loss of arousal, and 45 percent a loss of sexual response.

And when I talked to them, they were:

- » Perplexed—because they don't understand what's changed.

- » Disappointed—because they expected there to be more.

- » Frustrated—because they don't know what to do about it.

And when you carry those numbers from my practice to the rest of the country—well, more than 44 million women are aged 40 to 65 in the US alone. Some 6,000 of us reach menopause every day. And at least half of us experience sexual problems with menopause. Probably more.

That's a lot of disappointed women. And a lot of disappointed partners, too.

Women don't have to just accept the changes if they don't want to. From working with patients—and from my own experience as a midlife woman—I know there are steps that can be taken, products that can be used, that can help. When you reach 40, suddenly it's not easy to read the fine print. When that happens, will you give up reading? Of course not. You got reading glasses or bifocal contacts and went on. You adjusted.

But I found that many of my patients have little to no experience using sexual aids. I may recommend that they consider using a vibrator or a lubricant or a positioning pillow—but they have to actually purchase these things. I can just picture my patients walking out of my office and shaking their heads at the thought.

A majority of my patients are not going to visit a sex shop. They are not likely to be comfortable or happy visiting the sex shops online either. I looked and looked for a good place to send my patients, where the focus is on sexual health, on sustaining our sexuality. We need a safe place to shop, where the products are durable and made of safe materials. And frankly, we need a place that doesn't cast women as sexual toys, and that acknowledges a healthy sexuality for people over 40.

That led me to launch MiddlesexMD, a website for women like me and like my patients. We are from a generation of women who have redefined female sexuality, and are now redefining menopause. As pioneers, we all had a lot to learn, and still do. Through the website, my practice, and my growing network of medical colleagues specializing in this field, I've had conversations with hundreds of women about what we're facing, what we're hoping for, and what we wish we knew!

Along the way, I've published a blog responding to research I and the MiddlesexMD team (a wonderful collection of researchers, writers, therapists, physicians, and business thinkers) have come across and to questions women have asked me. What follows is a collection of those blog posts, especially selected for relevance to women looking to understand and take charge of what's happening in their sex lives.

I hope they're helpful to you as you navigate your own life, health, and sexuality.

Yes You Can: Dr. Barb's Recipe for Lifelong Intimacy

CHAPTER ONE

FACE THE CHANGE

It's a fact: as we get older, our hormone levels change. That means changes in our anatomies, sensitivities, and responsiveness. These are perfectly normal changes, and if we understand them, we can keep our bodies and minds in shape for continued sexuality. There are also plenty of things we can do to compensate for the changes, some of them quite simple, some requiring consultation with our health care providers.

I believe in the importance of intimacy in our relationships and the importance of individual sexuality as a component of our whole selves. And I know as both a physician and a midlife woman that the first step is to inform ourselves about what's happening now and what lies ahead.

KEEP ON LEARNING

Remember in middle school (we called it junior high in those days) when the boys and the girls were shepherded into separate rooms for those awkward films? It might have been presented by the gym teacher or the guidance counselor; maybe your school was large enough to have a health teacher who presided as we were introduced to the signs and effects of puberty—and the dangers of acting on urges.

My conversations with women lately have reminded me that while we take great pains to introduce our younger selves to their biology, we don't quite follow through. In the sex ed I'm familiar with, the story stops with the fertile years. We don't introduce the full cycle we can all expect to experience if we only live long enough.

Yes, breasts bud and menstrual cycles begin. We have children, or we don't; we may have illnesses or surgeries. At some point, the cocktail of hormones shifts, and the parts of our bodies once prepared for reproduction begin to change once more. Our periods become unpredictable and eventually stop (a year without defines menopause). Our tissues become dryer, more fragile, less elastic. Without care and attention—and often in spite of them—our vulvas and vaginas atrophy, which means they actually shrink.

And where do we learn this? Not in a gym or a cafeteria with a hundred of our same-sex classmates! For too many of us, we learn it only through our own experience, at a point in life when there aren't many people we're talking to about sex. We're tempted to think this is an odd thing that's happening only to us. We're a little embarrassed, maybe a little ashamed.

There's so much more common about our experience than most women think! If only there were a middle school for midlife, so we could all get together and learn about this next phase of physical transitions. As we thought (or it was hoped we were thinking) back in the original sex ed, knowing what's ahead is the first step in making good decisions and taking charge of our own sexual health.

This book, and the MiddlesexMD website, offer an alternative to the old sex ed approach which, I hope, will give you the information and encouragement you need to begin talking to your partner, doctor, and friends. Because even without the awkward films, we're all in this together.

LET'S GET AROUSED

This post was contributed by Julie, a member of the MiddlesexMD team.

Hi everybody. My name is Julie. I'm a writer here at MiddlesexMD. My credentials for writing about sex at midlife are… Well… I have reached midlife. And I enjoy sex.

Chapter One: Face the Change

Still.

Despite almost 30 years of togetherness with the same guy. Despite aches and pains, stress and too little time, and all the physical surprises of menopause. Despite all of that, we are nowhere near ready to hang up our sheets.

So when my own friend (we served undergraduate years together) and doctor (my own menopause doctor, because I'm lucky), Dr. Barb, asked me to help her develop her website, I jumped at the chance. I needed to learn about this myself. What better way?

I've been writing for years and years, and for many years researching and writing on health topics. But I have never written about sexual health. Barb is teaching me — you would not believe the size and density of these textbooks.

So, day one, lesson one, Basson's Model. I had no idea that there is a difference between Sexual Desire and Sexual Arousal. I really always thought they were the same thing, or flip sides of the same impulse, or something. Because that's the way I'd experienced it for most of my life. Arousal and Desire arrived on my doorstep, it seemed, instantaneously.

But they are considered distinct aspects of the sexual experience. And now that menopause has slowed me down a bit, I understand better.

We can achieve arousal with or without desire. We can have comfortable, enjoyable, emotionally satisfying sex with or without desire. That is, we need arousal for sex. But we don't need desire. We like it. We want it. We enjoy it. But we don't need it to engage in sex or get a lot out of our sexual experiences.

The easiest way for me to tease these ideas apart is this way: Desire happens in your head. It's an idea. Arousal happens all over. It's physical. Certainly the idea can spark a physical response. But it works the other way more often for women. Sexual stimuli — physical sensations, emotional feelings, sights, sounds, smells — arouse us physically. Our arousal readies our bodies for sex and can breed desire.

So, when we start talking about the kinds of sexual problems women may experience with menopause, the distinction becomes very important. Are we having difficulty with arousal or with desire? Or both?

What used to follow automatically from sexual stimuli — the arousal part — may now take more time and more stimulation. We may have to ask for and give ourselves more help and support to become aroused. This isn't a lack of desire, but a greater need for stimulation.

We may be receiving all the same sexual stimuli that we always have, that always worked before, but we don't respond to it as readily. We love our partners just as much or more. But our bodies just don't respond as quickly now. Or we may now have physical or emotional limitations or illness or medications that muffle the effect of sexual stimulation.

This was lesson one for me. A real eye opener. I used to worry that I didn't feel the same desire as I did when I was in my 20s and 30s. Worry isn't the word. It upset me. I am much more relaxed about it now. I'm learning to tune in to stimulation, to appreciate and notice my body's response more. And that helps a lot. Well, I suppose writing about sex every day doesn't hurt either…

There have been and will be many more lessons. Some embarrassingly basic. Some I wish I'd known 30 years ago. I will always be willing to show my ignorance in these matters, followed by Dr. Barb's patient teachings.

Meantime, I'm gathering up all my favorite stimulants: I'm with my friend Reka on the potency of Dr. Gregory House. And Dr. Andrew Weil too (his relaxation tapes have an opposite, unadvertised effect on me). I have a thing for David Strathairn. Indian food. Tango/dance movies. And I have this special drawer in my bedroom…. And you?

Chapter One: Face the Change

WHY WE LOVE ROSEMARY

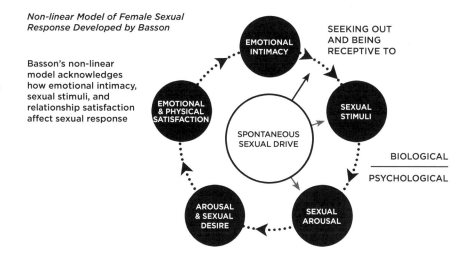

Rosemary Basson's model of female sexual response

The science of human sexuality is young. For most of the last century, we assumed that men and women approach sex in roughly the same way.

Older models (Masters & Johnson, Kaplan) theorized that sex for people happens in a few neat, linear stages, beginning with desire, proceeding next to arousal, then orgasm, and finally satisfaction.

But it doesn't always work that way, particularly for women, and especially for women over 40.

More recent researchers who focus on women's sexuality, confirm that really, women do not experience sex in this simple, linear way. We sometimes skip phases. Our reasons to have sex are many and often complex.

We can be perfectly satisfied with sex that does not include orgasm, and we can reach orgasm without desire. We are flexible that way.

Enter Rosemary Basson, MB, FRCP, of the University of British Columbia. Basson formalized a new model of female sexuality that is now widely accepted.

She offers two key insights. First: Female sexual desire is generally more responsive than spontaneous. That is, we are more likely to respond to sexual stimuli—thoughts, sights, smells, and sounds—than we are to spark an interest in sex out of thin air (Men, on the other hand, specialize in this).

Another key insight: emotional intimacy matters to women. That may not sound like a news flash, but in the realm of the biological sciences, it really is news.

So Basson drew a new model—not a linear series of steps, but a circle that includes both sexual stimuli — the thoughts that trigger a woman to take an interest in sex, and emotional intimacy—the emotional payoffs of the experience that lead her to want to come back for more.

I love Basson's model and use it every day in my practice to help my patients understand how sex really works for us.

We need to understand that it's okay and it's normal that we don't always start with desire. And as we enter menopause, and our hormone levels drop, spontaneous thoughts about sex, and responsiveness to opportunities for sex diminish for most of us. That's natural and normal too.

If you don't like the situation, and you want to feel more sexual, more responsive, Basson's model gives us the hint: We need to stimulate our minds. The more sexual stimuli we receive, the more sexual we feel.

So, this is worth thinking about today, a worthy discussion to have with your partner: What makes you feel sexy? A juicy romance novel? A James Bond movie? Erotic art? Pretty underpinnings? A romantic dinner? Having your partner empty the dishwasher? Spend some time thinking about that. Maybe make a list. And then provide for these things. Sexy is as sexy does.

OUR SECRET RECIPE FOR SEX AFTER MENOPAUSE

This post was contributed by Julie on behalf of the MiddlesexMD team.

The post title is just tongue-in-cheek, folks. A little health writing humor, poking a stick at the whole idea of health "secrets."

We don't believe in keeping information about attaining good health secret.

So here, today, we are happy to divulge our recipe for sex after menopause. The ingredients are:

» Knowledge

» Vaginal Comfort

» Pelvic Tone

» Genital Sensation

» Emotional Intimacy

Tada! Whooot!!! We have balloons falling and confetti rising over here at MiddlesexMD headquarters!! How about you?! No?

Wait, No?

Maybe you don't realize how hard it is to distill good-sex-after-menopause down to an easy-to-remember system? So let me explain: Months ago, we began our work with a hard look at the American Psychiatric Association's DSM-IV description of disorders contributing to Women's Sexual Dysfunction (There's a phrase we won't use a lot around here, because it worries us. If we don't yet understand Women's Sexual Function, how can we comfortably describe its dysfunction?).

We embraced (and strive to remain mindful of) the point of view of women's sexual problems developed by the New View Campaign, and their concerns about the medicalization of human sexuality. We reduced by our focus on peri-menopausal and menopausal women. We filtered all of these concerns through recent research and publications by members of the North American Menopause Society (NAMS) and the International Society for the Study of Women's Sexual Health (ISSWSH).

We surveyed current literature on female sexuality. We added recent work by sex researchers and therapists and coaches, relationship coaches and mindfulness gurus.

That was the first step.

The next step was sorting all of the helpful advice, tips, skills, and learning into clear descriptions of conditions and pragmatic actions so that women in menopause can understand exactly what is going on with their bodies and what they can do about it if they want things to be different.

We didn't go looking for the recipe. It surfaced from the work, organically. We began to see how all of the latest and best advice of medical, psychiatric, and sex researchers and coaches, seeking to help older women enjoy their sexuality, clustered into just a few central goals. What does a woman need to do to enjoy sex after menopause? (Assuming, of course, that she wants to enjoy sex after menopause at all. Because that is still her choice.)

KNOWLEDGE
She needs to know the physiology of menopause, so she understands what is happening when it happens, and especially that though her experiences are unique to her, she's not alone. And she needs to know some new sexual techniques that will keep sex enjoyable as she ages.

VAGINAL COMFORT
She needs to learn how to take care of her vulvo-vaginal tissues so that sex remains comfortable.

PELVIC TONE
She needs to learn how and why to strengthen and maintain her pelvic floor to encourage circulation and maintain or strengthen her orgasms.

GENITAL SENSATION
She needs to compensate for less blood flow and less sensitivity in her genital tissues by providing herself with more stimulation, more sexual sensation.

EMOTIONAL INTIMACY
She needs what every woman needs at every age for sex to be good. Sex needs to be intimate. It needs to mindfully create and reinforce a real connection.

There it is. No secrets. In this book and on our website, you can get all the rest: descriptions of conditions that get in the way of achieving these five goals, actions you can discuss with your doctor or take on your own to enjoy sexuality for life, and products we have selected to help you on your way.

BOOMER SEX: WE'VE GOT A LOT TO LEARN

When the results of a new AP-LifeGoesStrong.com poll of the boomer generation about sex and relationships were released in November 2010, the news media highlighted two seemingly contradictory findings, illustrated by these headlines:

» "Poll: Baby Boomers Sex Confident"

» "AP Poll Says Boomers Are Unhappy with Sex Lives"

The first story focused on the fact that the majority of people between the ages of 45 and 65 believe that they have "pretty much learned everything there is to know about sex." The second article reported on the percentage of boomers who say they are "dissatisfied" with their sex lives. Nearly a quarter—24 percent—of the 45-65 group said they were frustrated with their lovemaking (compared to 12 percent of 18-29 year olds and 17 percent of the 66-plus crowd).

Hmmm. I wonder if there's a connection.

My first reaction—and I speak as a medical doctor who specializes in menopause care and hears about the sexual lives of boomer women on a daily basis—is that I don't believe a person of any age can know everything there is to know about sex. In my experience, it's hard for a person to understand her own sexuality—how her body works, what she really needs and wants—and impossible for her to know everything about her partner's desires and expectations in the bedroom.

A closer look at the poll's results reveals a significant gender gap around these findings in the 45-65 age group. While 59 percent of boomer women said they know all there is to know about sex, only 48 percent of their male counterparts share that level of confidence. On the other hand, 48 percent of men age 45-55 said that their partners don't want to have sex as often as they do, while only 13 percent of women in that age group made the same complaint.

Sex therapist Dr. Ruth Westheimer, who helped develop the questions for the poll, says that the most important issue the findings highlight is that men and women in this age group have very different expectations in bed.

"We worry so much about teens and sex, but this poll indicates a need for a call to action for this segment of the population to become more sexually literate," she says. "It is not necessary for a couple to be in exact sexual synch, but if a couple's appetites grow too far apart, then that indicates that there is not enough communication about sex in the relationship."

Of course, communication is an essential component of satisfying sex. But I also wonder if what women who say they know everything there is to know about sex are really saying that they've lost interest in sex as they know it. That the kind of stimulation that excited and satisfied them when they were younger no longer does the trick. Real "sexual literacy" for both women and men at midlife requires knowledge about how our bodies are changing and what we can do to help each other have physically and emotionally satisfying sex lives as we grow older.

NOT TONIGHT, DEAR: WHY WE "DON'T FEEL LIKE IT"

We are complicated sexual creatures. For us, arousal isn't just a matter of plumbing; rather, it's intricately connected to how we feel about ourselves, our partners, and the rest of our lives. There is no "turn-on" pill; there is no magic potion. And while it's true that the way we experience arousal and sexual pleasure evolves and changes as we age, there's every reason to expect that our sexual experience can be even more relaxed, adventurous, and fun—just like the rest of our lives—if we pay attention to our overall mental and physical health. Because for us, the kneebone's connected to the thighbone—everything's connected.

This concept was brought home to me once again at a presentation I heard at the International Society for the Study of Women's Sexual Health (ISSWSH) by researcher Mara Meana, Ph.D. from the University of Nevada. Dr. Meana examined the reasons women might decide not to have sex, even if they were aroused and feeling sexual desire.

Of course, those reasons differ depending on the woman's life stage and personal situation, but what struck me was that the three main reasons that married women gave for avoiding sex were::

» Fatigue and the need to conserve energy

» Boring sex

» Negative body image

Sound familiar?

So, you may like having sex; you may be feeling aroused; you may be attracted to your partner, but you still avoid the time, energy, and emotional vulnerability of intercourse because of one or more of those three "disincentives."

Boredom, fatigue, and a negative body image are powerful ways to stifle that spontaneous, buoyant spirit we've so richly earned at this stage of life. I'd like to examine these disincentives in greater detail here and suggest some ways to overcome them. You'll also notice us returning to these themes throughout the book.

TOO TIRED! TOO MUCH TO DO!

Maybe the kids have flown the coop—or maybe not. Maybe your parents need more attention. Maybe you're still involved with your career; in fact, maybe you have a big presentation in the morning, and you need to be refreshed and on-point. Is it any wonder that sex is the last thing on your mind?

Life's demands ebb and flow, but they never go away. And your sexual self is closely connected to all the other flotsam and jetsam of your life. However, if your stress level and the demands on your time are chronic and overwhelming, other important parts of life, such as exercise, time to yourself, and intimacy with your partner are all too likely to fall quietly by the wayside.

Chronic stress, in addition to putting a terrible strain on your overall health, also interferes with the production of hormones that fuel libido. So, even though you may love and be attracted to your partner, lack of time and energy for sexual intimacy will cause that relationship to suffer over time. And, eventually, your desire for sex will diminish, too.

If the demands on your time and energy are draining away life's pleasures, it's time for some tough re-evaluation. The stresses may be unavoidable, like caring for elderly parents, but there's probably something you can do to ease the burden.

To really deal with the "too tired" state of affairs, you need to view your life holistically. Lack of time and energy for sex is only part of the picture.

Take care of yourself first. Carve out some space for emotional and mental rejuvenation, even if it's as simple as a warm bath or a night to yourself with nothing to do. But don't expect a one-time splurge to effect lasting change. Rejuvenation takes time and it takes conscious effort. How will you regain (or discover for the first time) your peaceful inner core?

Chapter One: Face the Change

» Take care of your health. If you don't have time for sex, chances are you're not paying attention to exercise or good nutrition, either. Among its many other benefits, exercise improves libido. It makes you more flexible, strengthens your joints, gets rid of aches and pains, and improves your mood. It makes you look and feel sexier. And, yes, all this takes time. Nobody said it would be easy.

» Talk to your doctor. Is it possible that fatigue is due to an overlooked physical condition? Could your medication be the culprit? Could you be depressed?

» And finally, pay attention to your partner. Rebuild the intimacy. Touch. Talk. Be creative. Sex doesn't have to be all-or-nothing. Enjoy the journey; the destination doesn't matter. Focus on pleasure, intimacy, and connection and the rest will likely follow. And yes, this takes time, too. Doesn't anything truly worthwhile?

There's no simple solution to dealing with stress and fatigue—or with their emotional and physical toll on your life. There's only the desire and commitment to change—to prioritize the most important things, which happen to be your health and your most important relationships. Because, after all those pressing demands on your time and energy have gone away, you'll either be spending much quieter years with a stranger you used to love or with your lover.

Change is hard, but the cost of the status quo, at this stage of life, is unacceptable.

SEX IS BORING.

"I can tell you the movements he's going to make step-by-step. He can get me off, but it's sex. It's not making love."
–quoted by Marta Meana, Ph.D.,University of Nevada, Las Vegas, "When Feeling Desire Is Not Enough: Investigating Disincentives to Sex"

If I had a nickel for every woman with this complaint, I could retire tomorrow. According to Dr. Meana and others who study female sexuality, boredom is the second biggest disincentive to sex in married women. But of all the sexual challenges, this one is the most fun—because the cure requires creativity, lightheartedness, and the willingness to play.

No matter how red-hot the passion once was, over time it's bound to cool to glowing embers. Left unattended for years, however, that flame will begin looking more like gray ash. Doctors and counselors—and your girlfriends—all have recipes for bringing the romance back into your relationship. I'm not trying to reinvent the wheel, but here are some suggestions I've gathered from various sources that look like fun to me.

I would, however, encourage you to take the initiative in this endeavor to reinvigorate your sex life. It's too easy to take a passive "hurry up and get it over" attitude. You're half the partnership, so you bear some of the responsibility for your love life. You can be more forthcoming with what feels good to you and what you'd like to try. I'm betting that your partner will be pleasantly surprised and willing to try.

1. Spend time together doing nonsexual things. For women "it's not what happens in the bedroom—their desire arises when they are interacting with their partner, just touching, talking, when they go on a hike or a picnic, that starts to get them sexually interested," said Patricia Koch, Ph.D., Associate Professor of Biobehavioral Health & Women's Studies at Pennsylvania State University. The first step, then, in rekindling the flame is to become romantically reconnected outside the bedroom.

2. Try self-stimulation. This may sound counterintuitive, but the idea is to "get your head in the game," not to create a substitute for sex as a couple. Sometimes masturbation can reignite that spark of sexual interest that leaves you wanting more.

3. Talk about what you like and what you want to try. As a more mature woman, you know what you want; you're more confident in asking for it. Maybe your partner has some idea to try as well.

4. Break the mold. No doubt, routine is boring. New places, positions, accessories, and techniques are an antidote to routine. Check out some romantic movies. Read an erotic book together. You're only limited by your imagination.

5. Keep it light. This should be a fun exploration, not a do-or-die ordeal. The goal is to expand your sexual repertoire as a couple, to pleasure each other, to reconnect both sexually and emotionally. You aren't trying to become sexual athletes or to experience orgasm every time.

So—boring sex? Not to be glib, but what a great problem to have. Its solution lies at least fifty percent in your hands.

HE'LL SEE ME NAKED!

The notion of body image has to do with how we feel emotionally about our appearance rather than how others view us or how we look objectively (height, weight, eye and hair color). It's a complex and many-colored concept that can be affected by things like past experiences (your mother's long-ago comment about your "cute pudge," for example, or, more difficult, sexual abuse), by cultural norms, by physical disease or injury, and by our own level of confidence and self-esteem.

According to researcher Marta Meana, Ph.D., negative body image is the third most common "disincentive to sex" for married women—even if we enjoy sex; even if we might feel like it at the moment. A negative body image is pervasive and potent. Many of us are embarrassed about our bodies to the extent that those feelings invade our most intimate relationships. Case in point: the woman whose husband, in 22 years of marriage, had never seen her naked body.

Granted, it takes a stout disposition to feel confident about our bodies in the face of our youth-crazed, celebrity-obsessed, skinny-jeans culture. Even when advertisers target a "mature" demographic, the models look like 30-year-olds with graying temples. The mantra that "50 is the new 30" perpetuates that unrealistic image against which real people like ourselves, with cellulite, love handles, saddlebags, sagging breasts, and fatty backs stand no chance.

However, for those of us who do manage to feel good about the way we look, it seems that a positive body image is strongly linked to more frequent and more satisfying sex. In at least one recent study, researchers at the University of Austin found "significant positive relationships between sexual functioning, sexual satisfaction, and all body image variables." Body image variables included things like weight concern, physical condition, and "cognitive distractions during sexual activity"—those irritating thoughts about our bodies that invade our intimate moments.

Another study of older women found that those who perceived themselves as less attractive also reported a decline in sexual activity. (They did, however, report that sex was still satisfying when they did engage in it.)

As we age, then, we're confronted with an opportunity and a challenge. While we may be more accepting, mature, and confident, we're also experiencing physical changes that are deemed undesirable by our culture. We can enjoy our evolving maturity and freedom, or we can cop to the cultural myth that labels aging unattractive and unsexy.

If you find yourself distracted by thoughts of your midriff rolls during sex or have the urge to dress–and undress!–in the closet, try these remedies:

- » Get naked in private. Walk around nude. Familiarity with your naked body might help you become more comfortable with it.

- » Get fit. No matter the size of your jeans, exercise makes you look and feel better. It's also a good way to become more aware of your body—and maybe more appreciative of how well it works.

- » Think positive. A survey conducted by Glamour magazine with Ann Kearney-Cook, PhD, revealed that most women think about their bodies negatively every, single day. And sometimes these thoughts are shockingly negative. This is powerful negative reinforcement. Be aware of your negative thinking and make an effort to break the cycle.

- » Practice acceptance. Self-confidence is a turn-on all by itself. There's nothing sexier than a woman who is comfortable in her own skin.

While making love with my partner I worried that he would see a hair here, or a flabby spot there, and be turned off. I noticed that he was never self-conscious about a skin blemish or when he gained a few pounds. So I started copying him and concentrated more on the sexual pleasure I felt. I began enjoying sex a lot more, and he noticed. He said it made him more excited, and the result? A great new circle of passion and sex.

>   –from Our Bodies, Ourselves: A New Edition for a New Era, 2005, Boston.

AN OPEN LETTER: HOW TO REALLY TURN ME ON

Dear beloved partner of mine:

We've been together for a long time. We've weathered some storms; we've had our ups and downs. The kids are raised; the house is ours again. These should be great years for us, right? That's why we need to talk. (I saw you cringe.)

You don't like to admit it, but things are changing for me. Yes, it's the change. The hot-flash and mood-swing change. The big M.

Maybe you've noticed that I don't lubricate as well during sex and that it takes me longer to become aroused. In fact, maybe you've noticed that I'm not "in the mood" much, or rather, I'm in a lot of moods, not all of them pleasant. That's because my emotions are on a trapeze, my body's changing, and so is the way I feel about sex and the way it feels to me.

And because I want our sex life to be fabulous in our golden years (I've read that after menopause, sex is often better than ever), I want to share some of the stuff I've learned. This may require some adjustment on your part, but in the interest of a happy, satisfied, sexy wife, it's worth it. Right?

Let's start with a little quote from a friend, influenced, I think, by Shakespeare: "Tup my mind and you can tup me."

There's a deep truth in that colorful nugget. Sex begins in our minds long before our bodies kick in. If you want good sex, here are some ways to get my mind in the game:

» Make me feel valued, desirable, beautiful. Maybe I've gained a few pounds; maybe I'm drenched in sweat at night; maybe I'm feeling old. But yours is the only opinion that matters to me. Look at me the way you used to. Bring me flowers. Tell me I'm beautiful—and mean it.

» Listen to me. Turn off the TV. Don't offer solutions. Don't try to fix things. Validate what I'm going through. Don't patronize me or belittle my experience. And don't even begin to think that it's "all in my mind." This is just a rough patch, and frankly, how sexy I'll feel toward you on the other end will have a lot to do with how attentive you are now.

» So—be attentive, just to be supportive, not for sex. Make dinner or clean up afterward. Leave a love note on the dresser or a sexy text on my cell. Do small things that let me know you're thinking of me. And not once or twice. Make this the new normal.

» Work out with me. I'm not happy with the way my body's changing. I don't feel sexy, and I don't feel confident. You can help by not only encouraging me to exercise and eat healthfully, but also by doing it with me. If we both diet and get in shape, think how much better sex will be—and maybe how much longer we'll have to enjoy it!

» Touch me. Just loving, compassionate touch without a hint of horniness. You know I'm a sucker for a good snuggle. You don't? Well, it's time you learned. A quick hug; a little shoulder massage after work; a nighttime cuddle—just to let me know you care.

» Be patient. You may be a magnet for my moods, and not the mood you're hoping for. Try to understand that my hormones have run amuck and that my body's playing tricks on me, and that you (certainly not my boss or my mother) are the safest target. I don't like it, either. Give me some space. Don't take it personally. If I was once a nice person, she'll be back, and she'll be very grateful for such a thoughtful, supportive partner.

» Be playful. Lighten up. Make me laugh. You don't have to be seriously funny, just be a little goofy. Laughter releases all kinds of soothing juju, and it reminds us that life is good.

» Educate yourself. Read this book and websites like MiddlesexMD.com so you have some idea about what's going on with my sexual apparatus. Then you can be on board when I suggest trying lubricants or sex toys.

With your support, I'm going to come out of this stronger, sexier, and more sure of myself than ever. We're in this together, Honey, whether you like it or not.

As gynecologist Dr. Don Sloan said, "The key to a woman successfully going through menopause is the quality of the support she gets from her husband, or the man in her life. The major mistake a woman makes is to think it's her problem, because she doesn't want to stress [her partner] out. There is no such thing as an uninvolved partner."

AN OPEN LETTER PART TWO: DOWN AND DIRTY

Dear beloved partner of mine:

If you read my last letter (you did, right?), then maybe you understand how I feel—and how to make me feel better—sexually speaking.

So let's stop beating about the bush. (Music to your ears, I know.) I'm going to get very specific about how to turn me on. But I'm hoping that if I take this step, you'll reciprocate, and maybe we can begin talking about sex more openly, about what we each like, and about how to make it good for both of us.

PRIME THE PUMP. Always remember that, for a woman, sex begins in the mind and imagination. Use that to your advantage. Begin early. Make the coffee and bring it to me in bed. Leave me a provocative note in the morning. Send me a sexy text. Bring home lovely wine and chocolate. Help me get my head in the game.

FINESSE THE FOREPLAY. I recently read that it takes a woman an average of 20 minutes to reach orgasm—and it takes a man four! Those numbers may be optimistic for both of us these days, but they illustrate one important difference between Venus and Mars: I need time! Besides, we're sitting on Golden Pond now. What's the rush?

Try starting in a different room. (Variety is always spicy.) Whisper sweet nothings. Tell me I'm beautiful. Show me that you desire me.

So once we get down to business, don't just go for the goal posts: tease me. Use light touch. Use your tongue. Use your imagination. Experiment. Try running your hands over my inner thighs, tickle my neck. Try stimulating my perineum. (That's the spot between my vagina and my anal opening.) Once I begin to steam up, hone in on the erogenous zones—my breasts and vulva. Lightly touch, lick, or kiss. Back off and do it again. Ask me to show you how I like to be touched.

MANY WAYS TO SCORE. Despite all you've heard about how hard it is for women to reach orgasm, we're actually equipped with several ways to do it. In fact, according to an article in Everyday Health, "researchers have even found a nerve pathway outside of the spinal cord, through the sensory vagus nerve, that will lead a woman to orgasm through sensations transmitted directly to the brain."

Pretty fancy, huh?

But the surest way to orgasm for most women is through the clitoris— it's the tail that wags the dog. And while it may take some practice to get it right, that little number isn't choosy about the medium. Both oral and manual stimulation work just fine.

I know you're not completely clueless, but let's run over some technique. First, remember the tease. Don't dive right in and go for gold. Kiss my abdomen and thighs, then move to the vulva and its inner lips. Gently lick or kiss. Explore with your tongue. Lick my clitoris lightly, then move away. Then come back. Don't lick one spot too intensely or too long, because it just becomes numb. Let me know you like this. Pay attention to how I'm responding. Do I seem to be getting turned on? You can ask, you know.

When I'm good and ready, you can focus on the clitoris. At this point, a firm, repetitive licking should do the trick. You can also place your finger in my vagina at the same time. Maybe you can find the elusive G-spot. I'll let you know. Or, you can caress my breasts as I'm coming into full-blown orgasm. You can also try to stimulate my perineum and see if I like that.

Another move (only slightly acrobatic) would be to move up to missionary (facing each other, you on top) when I begin orgasming clitorally and get your own orgasm started. (You should be pretty turned on by now—it's been more than four minutes.) It'll feel pretty good to me.

If this is a little overwhelming, or if you need more detail, I'll buy you the book *She Comes First: A Thinking Man's Guide to Pleasuring a Woman* by Ian Kerner.

GOOD POSITIONING. Finally, let's not neglect positions that might work better for me than our standard missionary. We could try what the kids call the "reverse cowboy," or the doggy-style, rear-entry position. Or maybe I could sit on your lap? That might hit some different nerve endings, plus we can get real cozy.

We could also try some pillows to help us get into all kinds of positions. (And to support our less-than-agile parts.)

And remember, if you've come and gone, and I'm still unsatisfied, we can always go back to the good old dependable clitoral orgasm. I just know how good you're going to get at it.

But really, honey, the point isn't to learn a bunch of new tricks, but to learn to accommodate our changing bodies and to have a more deeply satisfying time together.

And that's going to take some good communication and a lot of practice.

So, let's get started. I'll bring the lube; you get the wine and chocolate.

YOU NEVER KNOW: STAYING READY FOR SEX

I had a call the other day from a friend who's been a widow for several years. "I've found someone!" she told me, with just the slightest quiver in her voice. "I'm so excited I can hardly concentrate at work."

Of course I was happy for her—and happy that she called to set up an appointment with me for an exam in anticipation of resuming her sexual life. "I think everything's going to be okay," she said, "but I think I might want to come in and see you first so you can tell me for sure."

She did come in to see me and I was glad to be able to reassure her that, from a physical perspective, she was good to go. If I am able to place two fingertips in a patient's vagina without causing pain or discomfort, it's a good bet that she's going to be able to have intercourse comfortably.

But more than a few post-menopausal patients who come to my office have been astonished to discover that they can't pass the two-finger test. Their vaginal walls have narrowed and thinned over a period of time without regular intercourse, and I have to tell them it's going to take some work to get back into a condition where penetration will even be possible, let alone comfortable.

I run into this fairly frequently with women who are widowed and divorced at our stage of life.

They are grieving or angry—or both—and, without thinking too much about it, decide that their sexual days are behind them. Don't need to worry about that anymore! But, as my ecstatic friend can attest: You never know. Surprises happen, and when they do, it sure would nice to know that your body's ready and able to experience the pleasures of intercourse.

It's one of my biggest concerns for single women our age. If you're 30 when you divorce and 40 when you want to take it up again, there's been no lost ground. But if you're 50 and decide to resume sex at 60, it's a very different story. You find yourself in a new relationship, you're ready to be intimate, but your vaginal "architecture" has changed. It can be a very unhappy surprise.

Physical therapy with vaginal dilators can help to restore capacity for intercourse, but it's much simpler—and more pleasant!—if you don't lose that capacity in the first place. For all my patients and friends who are currently without partners, I recommend a "vaginal maintenance plan" that will help them keep their genitals healthy and ready for love: moisturize regularly; use a good lubricant; and experiment with a personal vibrator or dilator to preserve your capacity for penetration. (More on all this in the next section.)

Because you never know.

QUESTIONS... AND ANSWERS

Q: How long can perimenopause go on?

Perimenopause, also called menopause transition, starts with variation in menstrual cycle length. Cycles can go from every 28 to 30 days to every 21 to 24 days—or 21-40 days. Cycles that are closer, further apart, longer, shorter, heavier, or lighter are all considered normal for perimenopause. Rarely, women go from having regular periods to having none, skipping the "transition."

98 percent of women experience a natural menopause—one year without menstruating—between ages 40 to 58. I have seen one or two women at age 60 still menstruating—but somebody has to be that 1 to 2 percent! We really are unable to predict the age of menopause for any given woman. Again, for most women the symptoms of perimenopause last for four to eight years, but, again, there are a few stragglers who have them longer than most.

Any bleeding after menopause deserves investigation and evaluation, so it is important to differentiate post-menopausal bleeding from a few lingering periods.

I sense from the question that you're ready for a "change"! Hang in there. It's coming.

Q: Are mental fog and PMS-on-steroids related to perimenopause?

Oh, where do I begin? Perimenopause can be a pretty tough transition for many women. It is not only possible but probable that those symptoms are related. Patients with these complaints get a one-hour appointment in my practice to review the signs and symptoms that accompany this transition.

Riding it out is one option. Above all, make sure you optimize lifestyle, with exercise being probably the most important factor. Aerobic exercise of 45 minutes 5 days a week along with 60 minutes each week of strength training is a great goal to set.

I often recommend a book to patients: Dr. Robert Greene's Perfect Balance. It covers this transition quite well and reviews options in treatment including diet, exercise, and hormone alternatives. It was originally published in 2005, but is still one of the best I have seen.

Good luck! Things will get better!

Q: I'm not interested in sex at all. Is it all in my head, as my husband says?

A declining interest in sex as we age is typical for women, but many face a couple of additional factors that are really big: 1) It is painful; and 2) the event itself may not be particularly engaging. Is it any wonder that there isn't much motivation to participate?

If you have pain, you need to find a practitioner who can help solve that issue. There is almost always a solution for pain with intercourse. NAMS (The North American Menopause Society) is a good resource for finding a certified menopause practitioner if you feel your provider isn't able to find a solution–or you're not comfortable discussing the issue with him or her.

The other issue is more difficult to address. After years, maybe decades, of a less-than-fulfilling sexual relationship, it is hard to reinvent, but most women would agree it is worth trying. For some menopausal women a great sexual relationship doesn't even need to include vaginal penetration, but that takes a caring, nurturing partner.

Your partner needs to understand that romance and emotion are key to improving your libido–and you need to feel confident that you deserve that… because you do. For some women testosterone, in addition to that intimacy and foreplay, can make a remarkable difference in libido. Again, finding the right provider to investigate that option would be beneficial for you.

Some women have told me that visiting our site (MiddlesexMD.com) with their partners has been helpful. You might review the bonding behaviors together to start a conversation about what kind of foreplay and attention you need for a better opportunity for comfortable–even satisfying!–sex.

Your lack of interest is not in your head! I have yet to see a woman with pain with intercourse for which I couldn't find some cause and some solution options. Things to explore with a menopause care provider are atrophic vaginitis, vulvodynia, or vaginismus. Sometimes localized estrogen is required in addition to HRT to fully estrogenize the vagina.

There are solutions out there! Please explore them fully. Good luck, and don't give up!

Q: Can I regain my desire?

I wish there were a "secret sauce" that worked for all of us to restore libido. Not surprisingly, it's more complicated than that.

It's somewhat unusual to have an abrupt change to libido; for most women, it's a "slow drift." The first thing to consider with a dramatic change is any new or different medications. There are quite a few that have effects on desire: blood pressure, pain, and mood medications (antidepressants) to name a few. If you have had a change, you can work with your doctor to experiment with dosage or medications; let him or her know of this unintended side effect.

You ask about Cialis and similar products. They can help with orgasm (as they do for men), by arousing blood supply to the genitals, but they don't have an effect on libido or desire.

One option to consider is testosterone. While it's thought of as a male hormone, it's also present in women and is linked to libido. Some physicians aren't willing to prescribe it for women because it's an "off-label" use, but 60 percent of women report significant improvement in libido with testosterone replacement, and 20 percent of U.S. prescriptions for testosterone are now for women.

The other factor important to consider is mindfulness–which we might also call intentionality. While you may not feel desire that motivates you to be sexual right now, you know your long-time partner does. You can make the decision (together) that you will continue this activity together, including foreplay. (And I note a recent study that linked frequency of sexual activity with the quality of relationships, which confirmed my intuition.) When you make that decision, sex is a "mindful" activity: You anticipate and plan it and prepare physically and emotionally for an optimal experience with your partner.

Many women grieve the loss of a part of their lives that was once so important and fulfilling. It's most often an unnecessary loss, and staying sexually active has many health benefits as well as giving us feelings of both individual wholeness and connection to our partners.

Q: Can love lead back to desire?

First, let me assure you that you're not alone in feeling a loss of libido: It's common for women to lose desire, even in great, emotionally supportive relationships.

Low desire is challenging to treat, because we women are complex sexual creatures. I prescribe testosterone for some of the women in my practice; about 60 percent of those who've tried it have found that it does boost libido. I wish it were 100 percent, but it's not! And some physicians are reluctant to prescribe testosterone for women because it's "off-label."

Given what we know about women's sexuality, I advise women to engage "mindfulness" when it comes to sex. Often, we feel desire somewhere in the process of being intimate; we may not be driven to intimacy by desire. We need to choose to be sexual! I encourage women to plan for sex, committing to a frequency that is comfortable for both partners. It might be once a week, once a month, on Friday evening or Sunday morning—whenever you're least likely to be distracted, stressed, or tired. When we have been sexual, we've typically found it pleasurable and we're glad we did!

Finally, you mention being self-conscious about your breasts, which are no longer like they used to be. We are our own worst enemies when it comes to body image, and we pay the price when we rob ourselves of pleasures! I'll bet your partner doesn't look like he used too, either, and that he loves every inch of your body, as you love his.

CHAPTER TWO

INTENTION AND INTIMACY

Our sexual response is different from men's in a number of ways. We're more responsive than spontaneous. And we're more easily aroused by sexual stimuli if we start from a place of emotional intimacy.

One of the implications of our responsive nature is that we're less likely than either our younger selves or our partners to just, out of the blue, "feel like" having sex, no matter how much we enjoy it when we do! We need to decide whether sex is still important to us or to our partners, and then act on that.

At midlife, we can decide to rediscover the intimacy we experienced earlier in our relationships, or to engage emotionally for the first time. Whatever our earlier sexual experience, we can have the best sex of our lives--for as long as we like.

WHAT SUBTRACTS MORE THAN IT ADDS?

That sounds like a bad riddle, right? Like one I heard on NPR last week: What goes up a hill and down a hill but doesn't move? The answer to that one is a road. And the answer to what subtracts more than it adds is sex.

Here's the disturbing—but not, when I think about it, surprising—statistic I ran across this week, courtesy of colleague Sheryl A. Kingsberg, a PhD and chief of the Division of Behavioral Medicine at the University Hospitals Case Medical Center: "When sex is good, it adds 15 to 20 percent additional value to a relationship. When sex is bad or nonexistent, it plays an inordinately powerful role draining the relationship of positive value—about 50 to 70 percent!"

I was so struck by that statistical picture, I'm on the trail of the original research to understand more. But in the meantime, what I know from other studies—and my own experience and conversations with women—suggests that's about right.

Let me first say that good sex doesn't automatically make a relationship good. And a good, loving relationship doesn't automatically mean that the sex will be good. But if I think back to a study done a couple of years ago, "The Components of Optimal Sexuality," I'm reminded of how many of the characteristics of good sex are also characteristics of good relationships.

I won't revisit the whole list (read the detail about it in the last section of this book), but here are just a few that come to mind in this context:

- » Being present. It's so easy to take our partners (and, of course, others in our lives) for granted. Truly paying attention to one another—today—is a great gift.

- » Connection. When we feel connected to our partners, intimacy comes naturally (especially when we're overcoming obstacles together). If you're feeling "together but alone," there are steps you can take.

- » Authenticity. At this point in our lives, I find that many of us are more willing than ever to own what we think and feel. Whether we're in long-standing or new relationships, this helps us to be ourselves—and to be open about what we like and need, in the bedroom and the rest of life.

- » Vulnerability. Having sex is perhaps the ultimate act of making yourselves vulnerable to each other. What a reinforcement of the bond that a couple has with each other!

If those parts of your relationship are important to you, too, you've got more reason to understand how to stay healthy and be intentional about nurturing this part of your life.

WHAT IS A HAPPY MARRIAGE?

Recently, I saw an article about the link between sexual intimacy and marital happiness. The research, by Adena M. Galinsky and Linda J. Waite, found that continued healthy sex-lives help couples dealing with physical illness, especially chronic health problems.

Couples who had sex frequently (and sex was defined broadly—it didn't need to include vaginal intercourse) were more likely to say they had a good relationship.

This is, of course, a chicken and egg problem: More sex doesn't automatically make a relationship good. It's more likely—and perfectly reasonable—that an unsatisfying relationship will include less sex. And the women I meet through my practice as well as the rest of life show me that midlife is often a time when our relationships get some re-evaluation. Different couples will face different challenges.

Sometimes it's the empty nest, and the change in schedules and priorities that comes with it. Sometimes it's retirement, for one or both partners, which means a lot more together time. Sometimes it's the stress of caring for aging parents along with everything else. Whatever the prompt, when some of us look at our relationships, we say, "Is this really what I want?"

So it was interesting to me to read the details of the Galinsky Waite study, to see how they measured the quality of relationships. These are the questions they asked:

» How close do you feel your relationship with your partner is?

» How often can you open up with your partner if you want to talk about worries?

» How often can you rely on your partner for help with a problem?

- » How often does your partner make too many demands?
- » How often does your partner criticize you?
- » How happy is your relationship with your partner?
- » Do you like to spend your free time together, separately, or some of both?
- » How emotionally satisfying is your relationship?
- » How often does your partner get on your nerves?

If you're feeling some vague discontent, those questions might help you with a conversation with your partner—or with a couples therapist if you decide some outside perspective and coaching would be helpful. If you're feeling angry, or resentful, or isolated in your relationship, it's no surprise that you're not feeling sexy.

And you deserve to.

ROMANCE AWARENESS MONTH? SEIZE THE DAY

The editor of the MiddlesexMD newsletter, who somehow knows these things, tells me that August is Romance Awareness Month.

Who knew?

According to an online poll by Zoosk, which calls itself a "romantic social network," couples enjoy more romance than single people. Without getting too fussy about the details, according to the Zoosk survey, 79 percent of people in couples say that their partner is romantic while only 41 percent of single people say the same (presumably of their current interest?).

And even though the vast majority (78 percent) of those polled consider romance important in a relationship, only 20 percent of single people are happy with the romance in their lives compared to 59 percent of the coupled folks.

(Just to be clear, neither single people nor couples considered taking out the garbage romantic—so don't try to make that count.)

In honor of Romance Awareness Month, maybe it's time to take stock of the romance in your life. Are you stuck in a rut? A little rusty when it comes to new ways to woo your honey? Or maybe you haven't thought about romance in a long, long time.

Romance might be considered a nuisance and a bother by some long-term couples. Romance is for newlyweds. What's the point? He (or she) knows I love him (or her).

Maybe. But we frail human creatures still need reassurance from time to time. And saying the words out loud keeps our own emotional machinery in good working order, too. I'm betting that couples who manage to stay sexy and in love over the years are very good at romance. You know the couples I'm talking about. They hold hands; they enjoy being together; they touch; they make eye contact.

Romance can be as simple as a little squeeze or an "I love you" before bed. In fact, couples in the Zoosk survey actually preferred a hug and a kiss to dinner by candlelight (41 to 39 percent), while the singles prefer the dinner to the kiss (44 to 32 percent).

The tricky thing about romance is that it requires you to really know your partner in order to anticipate the unique things that will please him or her. Roses and chocolate might completely miss the mark while fresh coffee in the morning might be the most sensitive, loving and, yes, romantic, gesture imaginable. There's no one-size-fits-all when it comes to romance.

Romance is all about acts of thoughtfulness and caring that is uniquely targeted toward the person you love. It's about going a little out of your way for no reason at all, except that you care.

Done right, romance communicates to your partner that he or she is uniquely loved, and that leads to a sense of intimacy and caring in return. (And maybe to sex.)

This is the stuff that keeps a relationship tender and vital. While romance can be sexy, it isn't about sex; it's about expressing your love without ulterior motive or expectation of return in a manner that that only your partner will appreciate.

August may be Romance Awareness Month, but there are eleven more months to practice in.

Let's get started!

A LITTLE CONVERSATION ABOUT MINDFULNESS

Since launching MiddlesexMD, I have to say, my dinners have gotten a lot more spicy.

You know how it is when dining with buddies. It's polite—required—for them to ask what you've been up to lately.

When I tell them about MiddlesexMD, you would think it might stop the conversation cold, but I've found just the opposite is true.

My friends do want to talk about this. It's not surprising when men are there that they are a bit more quiet, but they are engaged, too. We all appreciate our partners' attention to these discussions—because we're not always alone with these changes. They affect our sexual partners, of course.

I had dinner the other night with an old friend. The subject of our conversation turned to the idea of how important it is, especially for long-partnered people, to keep their sexuality top-of-mind if they want to keep their sex life going. I talked about how older women, particularly, need extra stimuli (both physical and emotional) as they get older.

We need more opportunities to think about sex, consider it, fantasize about it, and more deliberate acts of intimacy when it's possible throughout the day to find or sustain the mood. Sex is like any pursuit: If you want to get better at it, it requires your attention. Some call this "work" Awareness or Mindfulness. And I think this dimension of a relationship is valuable enough to "do the work." (Smile.)

It was a simple conversation. I didn't think it had any sort of profound effect at the time. But I ran into that friend a few weeks later. She pulled me aside, and whispered, "Hey Barb! Thinking about sex more? It works!"

I wasn't surprised, if it works for me, it should for you too!

Gee, I love my job.

MAKE TIME STAND STILL: THE BODY SCAN

This post was contributed by MiddlesexMD team member Julie.

I'm busy exploring the boundaries of a new phase of my life, brought on by an illness I'm managing. As illnesses will, it's grabbed me by the collar, given me a big shake, and forced me to order my priorities. Also, it's made me take a good look at Time.

Not in the Time-is-Limited sort of way, but in the nature of time. How fast it goes when we're not paying attention, or when we are multitasking, when we're playing our To Do lists in an endless loop in our minds. And how it's actually possible to slow it down when we are paying careful attention to what we are doing.

I first noticed this in a not-so-pleasant way, as a young girl, in bed with horrible headaches. These headaches made me seek out darkness and quiet, and there was very little that medications could do to reduce the pain. I would lie for hours in bed in an eyemask, and the hours felt like days. I could think of very little else besides the pain, and time stood still.

It wasn't until I tried meditation for the first time that I had the experience again—meditation made time stand still. This was in the 70s, and through the PBS television series, Lilas Yoga and You. Remember lovely Lilas? She ended most classes with Savasana. It was through her suggestions during savasana that I first learned to do a "body scan," a way of getting in touch with my body through guided meditation.

In Body Scan meditation, you begin in a relaxed state, then use your mind to 'visit' every part of your body, noting how it feels, acknowledging pain or stiffness or itchiness, lightness or heaviness. It's a way of checking in with your body, to connect with it. It sounds simple, but it does take practice. You can use body scan to help you relax. You can use it to help manage pain.

That work, inadvertently, taught me to manage the pain of my headaches from a very early age. I learned to separate the pain I experienced in my head from the rest of my body. I learned to relax into the pain, and keep it sequestered from the rest of my body. I thought I'd discovered some secret power, until I came upon the work of Jon Kabat-Zinn. What I'd stumbled upon through Yoga, he'd been teaching for years through his Stress Reduction Clinic at the University of Massachusetts Medical Center.

By now you must be asking yourself how any of this ties into midlife sex. Well, my secret power, savasana and body scan meditations, also taught me to relax and enjoy sex. I've always been a woman who wished for a body different from the one I had, so early experiments with sex were always fraught with efforts to conceal from my lover the parts of my body I didn't like. That kind of distraction is a real barrier to intimacy.

Later, mindfulness techniques helped me to turn off the chattering brain brought on by an overstuffed life, at least during lovemaking.

Now, mindfulness helps me to stop the clock during lovemaking. It helps me keep the pain in my body contained so that it can't overwhelm the experience of lovemaking. And it helps me to fully appreciate my one and only body. The only one I'll ever have. Might as well love it.

If meditation can make time stand still, can stop the clock, might as well try it, right? If you've never tried meditation, you should know it's not that hard to learn, and not that easy to master. It's one of those things that just gets better with practice. And I know of no better or less intimidating guide than Kabat-Zinn, especially through his Mindfulness for Beginners program.

SEX: DECIDING TO JUST DO IT

We are learning more and more about what motivates women to have sex—enough to know that we still don't know that much.

We do know that our motivations change with our situations. What motivates us when we're young and single is very different from what motivates us when we're older, and in long-standing relationships, or older and single.

So when we suffer from lack of desire—are we missing the sort of drive we had when we were teenagers? And is it possible we just haven't found a new motivation for sex?

The more we learn from women, the more it seems that for us sex doesn't always begin with lust, but instead starts in our hearts and minds. We engage in our heads first, decide to have sex, and then with enough mental and emotional stimulation, our genitals respond. The older we grow, the more this is true. Age and maturity bring a new game into the bedroom.

For us, having sex is less an urge than a decision. One we can choose to make and then act upon. When we decide to say yes instead of no, decide to schedule sex instead of waiting (perhaps for a very long time…) for our body to spontaneously light on fire, decide to engage with media or methods that will put us in the mood rather than wait for romantic moments to happen along, we're using our heads to keep sex in our relationships.

Deciding to be intimate unlocks the pleasure. And the more sex we decide to have, the more sex we will feel like having. That's the secret to regular bonding.

Why just decide to do it? This much we know:

» Sex leads to a longer life.

- » Sex, like all exercise, helps protect us against heart attack and possibly stroke.

- » Hormones released during sex may decrease the risk of breast cancer and prostate cancer.

- » It bolsters the immune system.

- » Sex before bed helps us get to sleep.

- » Of course, sex burns calories.

- » Sex can help relieve chronic pain, including migraines.

- » An active sex life is closely correlated with overall quality of life.

- » Good sex can protect us against depression.

- » Good sex reduces stress and increases self-esteem.

- » Sex with your significant other stimulates feelings of affection, intimacy and closeness.

Making sex a focus in your life as you get older doesn't make you unusual. A study by AARP found that 66% of women age 45-59; 48% of women age 60-74 and 44% of women over the age of 75 believe that a satisfying sexual relationship is important to their quality of their life.

We think those numbers would be higher if women knew they could engage in thoroughly satisfying sex without waiting around for desire. Just by using their heads.

WARMING UP TO FOREPLAY

I'm a recreational runner, and before a run, I always spend a few minutes warming up. I'll do some stretches and walk a short distance. Experts no longer say this is a must, but I do it anyway because I know that as I've grown older, I have tighter muscles and less range of motion in my joints. And I've learned that if I exercise and end up hurting, I'll be more likely to postpone my next outing.

This cycle can also be true of sex. If you rush past the warm-up—foreplay—you may not have enough lubrication to make penetration comfortable. If sex hurts, you're less likely to initiate it or to respond to your partner. The more time that passes without having sex, the more difficult it is.

Many couples have a long habit of foreplay, but if the women I talk to are representative of the larger population (and I believe they are), men don't always get the connection. They are happy to skip the foreplay and sprint to the finish line. Early in the relationship, that might work even for women, who are more sexually complex than men, because excitement is high all the way around and it's easier to get aroused. It might even fly during the "thirsty thirties," when women's sexuality peaks.

But during menopause and after, hormones work against us. Estrogen declines, vaginal tissues become thinner and more fragile, and circulation to those tissues decreases. The less stimulation your vagina receives—from sex with a partner or your own self-care—the faster those changes happen. We're not kidding when we say, "use it or lose it!"

So after menopause, we need more to warm up. More real intimacy, more talk, more titillation. In short, more time. The stakes are higher now. If we don't warm up, it hurts. If it hurts, we don't want it. If we avoid it for too long, it's more and more difficult to have it. If any of this sounds familiar, it's probably time to talk about it.

Because a little foreplay has gone a long way in the past, your partner might be puzzled when you suggest your lovemaking include more foreplay. He might worry he's losing his sexual prowess. This is a great opportunity to explain how changing hormones affect your response to sex. If there's something you've secretly been longing to suggest to him lo these many years, you can slip that into the discussion, too. It's never too late for your partner to learn, and telling him what you need and why is a great first step.

Chapter Two: Intention and Intimacy

SATISFACTION: IT WORKS BOTH WAYS

I saw a patient this week who is in her early 60s, in great shape, and happily married to an attractive and generally healthy man also in his 60s. Recently retired from executive positions, they have been traveling to exotic — and romantic! — locales, enjoying fine cuisine and luxury accommodations.

They haven't had sex in two years.

My patient told me that her husband had started having problems maintaining an erection since beginning medication for hypertension. After a series of failed attempts at their usual way of making love, they had given up trying to have intercourse. When I asked her if they pleasured each other sexually in other ways, using oral or manual stimulation for example, she simply shook her head.

This female response to male erectile dysfunction—not an unusual one by any means—intrigues me.

When the female half of an otherwise healthy, happy, heterosexual couple experiences a condition that prohibits penetration, she is typically eager to explore other options for sexual intimacy. But it doesn't seem to work the other way. It's like if he's not going to get the ultimate end result—orgasm—then neither of them are.

I suspect what happens is that when men have difficulty performing, they start initiating sex less often. So once a week becomes once a month, and then there's a problem and three months go by and it doesn't work that time either, and—then it's done!

What's up with that, ladies? Do partners with erectile dysfunction really lose all interest in any type of sexual intimacy? Or is it just hard—for both of you—to change the game plan, the way sex happens, the way it starts, the way the "end result" is achieved or defined?

My guess is that many of these men would welcome their partners' attempts to change things up, to experiment with new techniques and sensual aids that can enhance pleasure on both sides.

IS SLEEPING APART THE END OF SEX?

People often make jokes about snoring (the word itself is kind of funny), but if you're losing sleep because your partner is a loud snorer, you know it's anything but humorous. Not only are you fatigued the next day, but that often leads to feelings of resentment, which is hard on the relationship, especially over time.

There are lots of remedies available for snoring, but if none of them work, what do you do? Or what if you can't agree on the temperature of the bedroom or the depth of the blankets—you're hot and your partner is cold? You work different schedules or your internal clocks put you to sleep or wake you up at different times?

A lot of women at this stage of life choose to move into a different bedroom, especially if the kids are gone. And while that may be a good solution for a good night's sleep, what does it do for their sex lives?

There's nothing more intimate than sleeping together. But if you can't just roll over and initiate sex, will it still happen?

The answer is, yes. But it might require a little more work. You may have to become more conscious about having sex, and that can be a good thing. It might mean you cuddle up while you're watching a sexy movie on TV. Or move your partner's hand somewhere intimate while you're sitting together on the couch.

Indeed, not sleeping together may actually rekindle some of the passion and make sex more exciting. It might also keep you from taking it for granted. Because it's true what they say about absence making the heart grow fonder. If your partner isn't so readily available anymore, it might actually make you want intimacy more often.

So not sleeping together does have its benefits (including the fact that you'll feel a lot better once you start getting a good night's sleep!)

The important thing is to keep the fires burning one way or another. Don't allow not sleeping together to become an issue or get in the way of having a healthy sex life. Instead, use it to your advantage.

Talk about it with your partner and communicate your true feelings: It's not about him; it's about getting a good night's sleep. And if your relationship is good, things might even improve in that area.

YOUR HOUSE IS NOT YOUR OWN?

Today, more and more women over age 50 are finding themselves sharing their households with parents and/or grown children. A recent article in the Atlantic magazine, "Grandma's in the Attic, Junior's in the Basement," talks about the big jump in multi-generations living under one roof, from grandpa or grandma who move in to adult kids who move back.

The article cites a recent Pew Foundation study estimating that 16 percent of the U.S. population now lives in multi-generational households—the largest share since the 1950s. Reasons range from economics to caring for elderly parents.

These findings made me think about how complicated it can be for women in that situation to keep their sex lives alive and kicking. If you're married, having a romantic evening (let alone having sex) presents all kinds of logistical problems. Knowing that your 78-year old mother is in the next room is not exactly an aphrodisiac.

If you've got grown children around, they can be even worse: Even a hint of parental romance can still gross them out (although they should know better!)—and curtail any action on your part.

To make matters worse, this multi-generational living may not have been your first choice; it may be happening just when you were starting to really enjoy being alone with your partner again, comfortably settling in as empty nesters.

So what's a sexually active, post-menopausal woman to do? Make an effort, that's what.

Go on an overnighter every few months, even if it's just to the hotel downtown. Or ask friends if you could borrow their cabin in the woods some weekend.

Yes, it might take some planning ahead, but that in itself could be exciting (as those Viagra ads imply). So when grandma goes to visit your sister and your kids are out on their dates, make your own date to "meet in the bedroom" once the coast is clear.

Or be spontaneous and grab any moment that presents itself. Make a game out of it.

The point is, if you have a healthy sex life, don't let these new circumstances ruin it for you. Good sex is not something to let casually slip away. And the way to keep it is to keep at it, making a commitment to get together in spite of your situation. Make it a priority; put it at the top of your "Things to do" list once in awhile!

Because, remember, having a good sex life is good not just for your relationship but for your overall health. If you do get caught by an older or younger resident, tell them you were just "exercising"!

MOVIES TO TURN YOU ON

Not long ago I spent a movie night with girlfriends, exploring erotica and talking about what sort of flicks worked to turn us on. I was motivated (honest!) by the premise that as we grow older, using movies and literature and images to "get in the mood" can really help us overcome our skimpy sex hormones to fire up libidos.

Out of that conversation, we compiled a list of movies that we found hot or naughty or disturbingly sexy, and a friend wrote asking for details on the movies we chose. Here's a bit about each of them:

A Room With a View
Romance literature depends upon eras when a lot of clothes, social restrictions and sexual oppression offer the perfect fuel to set off explosive passion. Helena Bonham-Carter and Julian Sands' longing is by turns sweet and frustrating, and always titillating.

Breathless
If you have a tendency to fall for bad boys, Jean-Paul Belmondo is your type. A liar and a thief and a persistent seducer. The film is set in Paris,

a classic and masterpiece of the influential director, Jean-Luc Godard and writer Francois Truffaut.

9 1/2 Weeks
Mickey Rourke and Kim Basinger are just bad for each other, and it's so good. Lots of erotic play. Lots of sex. A terrible relationship. Not so much a feel-good movie here. You don't hope they end up together in the end. New uses for the jars of stuff in your fridge.

Body Heat
William Hurt and Kathleen Turner in a steamy southern summer film noir. She seduces him, talks him into murdering her rich, oppressive husband so they can live happily ever after. The seduction and heat and sweat between these characters is more than memorable.

The Piano
A movie pairing Holly Hunter and Harvey Keitel made our list of sexiest films? Oh, my, yes. A haunting story of passion and the bargains women make to survive, and to thrive.

Atonement
The lovely, epic novel about class, love, jealousy, malice, and regret is made alive with performances by Keira Knightley and James McAvoy, whose passions are doomed from the start. But they do get off to a good start...

Shakespeare in Love
Find just about anything with a Fiennes in it—Joseph or Ralph—and you'll likely find a hot film. These boys embody sexuality. Here Joseph is the young Shakespeare, and he's in love. Gwyneth Paltrow is Viola, a woman mismatched and thwarted. A funny movie with a Shakespearean plot and much of his dialogue. The heat between Fiennes and Paltrow is luscious.

The Unbearable Lightness of Being
Daniel Day-Lewis, Lena Olin, Juliette Binoche. The cast should be enough to recommend the film. The sexy and disturbing triangle of Milan Kundera's novel, gorgeous Prague, the Soviet invasion. This is one beautiful, erotic, memorable film.

Looking for Mr. Goodbar
Diane Keaton and Richard Gere are hot for each other, and the movie made our list of turn ons for that reason. But their obsessions get the best of them, to say the least. Amazing performances by great actors.

Sweet Land
Elizabeth Reaser and Patrick Heusinger are awkward and beautiful as they work his rural Minnesotan farm. A gorgeous movie whose sensuousness bubbles up from nowhere and nothing. There are so many barriers to this romance, it just has to bloom. And it does. And it's breathtaking.

The Graduate
Dustin Hoffman loves Katharine Ross and lusts for her mother, Anne Bancroft. Sick? Well, yes, okay. Yes. And really, really sexy too. 60s angst. Remember 60s angst? We do.

Under the Tuscan Sun
The title gives it away: Tuscany. Heat. This film is about escape and discovery. A grown woman's fantasy come true.

Thief of Hearts
Sexy Steven Bauer has stolen Barbara Williams' diary. Her dull and predictable life breeds a rich fantasy life in those pages, and now he knows every detail of it. Careful what you wish for, girlfriends...

Vicky Cristina Barcelona
Javier Bardem could stand in the middle of the room and read our grocery list, and that would be enough for us. But put him in a movie with a lot of sexy women and supremely sensuous surroundings, and... why aren't there more movies like this?

Moonstruck
Ah, Moonstruck. How many times have we seen it? A dozen times? How many media have we owned it in? VHS, Disc, DVD, Digital... and counting... This campy romantic comedy just never gets old. An aging Italian Cinderella in Manhattan gets another chance at love. And she takes it. Cher and Nicolas Cage. Mama Olympia Dukakis nearly steals this movie.

Daniel Craig films
Oh Sigh. His Bond flicks are so yummy. But really, we'll take him in anything, in or out of a tuxedo. Out is good.

HITTING THE SEXUAL "RESET" BUTTON

Maybe your last child left home, as mine just did this fall. Maybe you (or your partner) retired. Maybe your partner became ill. The catalyst could be one of many life events, or it could simply be the realization of time passing, but at some point you look at your partner and realize that you'll be spending the rest of your lives alone together.

Do you need to hit the "reset" button?

Life passages tend to elicit examination and reassessment. These bittersweet moments give you an opportunity to readjust and re-evaluate. They give you a second (and third, and fourth...) chance to get things right. You tend to be more receptive to feedback and direction during those times. You tend to be less complacent.

Chances are that after years of distraction—raising a family, building a career—your relationship needs some attention, and that includes the sex. "Sex is always where the grit of a relationship settles," writes a reader to the UK's Globe and Mail. In that sense, sex is like the canary in the coal mine—an early warning system that all may not be so copacetic in the relationship.

So, how is your sex life? Robust and satisfying? Routine and uninspiring? Or is it non-existent? If your answer falls into the "boring" or "non-existent" categories, it's time to reset.

"When sex drops off there's a lot more at stake than missing out on pleasure," says Joan Sauers, author of Sex Lives of Australian Women. "A healthy sex life is critical to the survival of a relationship. Without it, our happiness and overall health can suffer."

Begin with reflection. Is infrequent, boring, or non-existent sex perhaps an indication of deeper trouble—entrenched lack of communication, trust, or respect? Is it due to physical changes or limitations that you haven't risked discussing? In this case, hitting the "reset" button should include some honest soul-searching with your partner and maybe some sessions either with a sex therapist or a marriage counselor. Simply addressing the sexual issues without tackling the underlying problem is like painting over rotten wood. The veneer won't hold for very long.

However, working to improve your sex life ipso facto improves the relationship as well, because both rely on intimacy, connection, and communication. "Keeping things interesting outside of the bedroom also plays an important part in keeping things exciting in the bedroom," writes Rhegan Lundborg, sex and relationships expert for the Omaha Examiner. "Doing new and fun things completely outside of the bedroom can be a great way to reconnect emotionally as well as take sole focus off the sex and just spend time enjoying each others company."

Focus on reconnecting. In a quiet, intimate surrounding, reminisce about the day you met, your first kiss, what attracted you to your partner. Go through a photo album together. Talk about key moments in your relationship—adventures you shared, challenges you got through. Few people in your life know you as well as this person. That's a rare and precious treasure. Make time to appreciate it.

From memories, move on to fantasies. In a perfect world, what would you like to accomplish or experience together—or separately? What's still important?

Don't be stingy with the sugar. Express approval. Say thank you. Notice the small ways your partner is thoughtful.

It takes time and careful tending to reignite a flame. As you rebuild intimacy on other levels, communication about your sexual connection could follow naturally. Or you may have to initiate the conversation when the time is right. Or—you may have to initiate the conversation with professional help.

Start the conversation in a safe, accepting, non-judgmental space. You both are likely to be experiencing changes, whether physical or emotional. You may have fears; you may be vulnerable. And you may also have fantasies—things you'd like to try but never had the guts to ask.

Isn't it time to hit the "reset" button and get this conversation started?

PRAYER AND SEX: NOT SUCH STRANGE BEDFELLOWS

I had never thought of bringing together these two very personal and powerful actions until I read an article by psychotherapist and MiddlesexMD advisor Mary Jo Rapini. She writes, "One method not as well studied but also valid in bringing a couple closer together and improving sex lives is prayer."

Well, that got my attention! Prayer, however you express it, has always seemed like something you do alone and in private, although we pray with others in certain contexts, such as liturgies and church rituals.

Sex, on the other hand, is an intimate and private act between two people, who may sometimes struggle with the vulnerability such intimacy demands.

But bringing the two together? Doesn't that seem, um, odd if not downright sacrilegious? After all, one is sacred and one is, um, fairly creaturely.

Actually, prayer and sex are the most natural intertwining of intimate acts in the world.

If you believe in any sort of Higher Power, bringing that Being consciously (through prayer) into your sex life could open a new level of intimacy between you and your partner. It could also sweep away those musty, Victorian notions that sex is somehow "of the flesh" and therefore opposed to things of the spirit. Which may be where that stubborn scent of guilt that clings to sex originates.

Nothing could be further from the truth. There is no such dichotomy, even though we tend to create one. Male and female become "one flesh"—that's how we were made, to be sexed creatures. We were made this way by the God whom we would prefer to exclude from the bedroom.

"See, sex in not an afterthought, a way to make more babies. Rather, it is an indispensable quality woven in the fabric of each life on this planet. Sex is not first something we do; it is primarily who we are," writes Dan Hayes about sex and prayer.

Why not invite God in? Consciously. By praying together. You don't even have to belong to the same religion—you just have to believe. (God is there anyway; it's just helpful for us to acknowledge it.)

Sex is a sacred act. That concept is the foundation of many Eastern practices, such as the Tantra. Sex is sacramental—the most intimate physical joining that human creatures can attain. Prayer acknowledges this, and it introduces a different kind of intimacy and perspective between partners.

A few of the effects of bringing prayer into sex, according to Mary Jo, are that by acknowledging a higher power, our own ego and self-righteousness dissolve, unspoken barriers between partners are broken down, and the bond between them is strengthened.

Praying together begets acceptance and forgiveness. It softens the sharp edges that creep into a relationship over time.

So, in the midst of using all the other tips and tricks we've discussed so much on this site, why not also pray together? You can do it in any way that's comfortable for you. You don't have to use words, but it might be helpful for each of you to hear the prayer of the other.

Join hands. Be still. Quiet yourselves.

Then pray. Together. With or without words.

If you don't know what to say, here's a starter:

Father, send your Holy Spirit into our hearts. Place within us love that truly gives, tenderness that truly unites, self-offering that tells the truth and does not deceive, forgiveness that truly receives, loving physical union that welcomes.

Open our hearts to you, to each other and to the goodness of your will. Cover our poverty in the richness of your mercy and forgiveness. Clothe us in our true dignity and take to yourself our shared aspirations, for your glory, forever and ever.

("A Prayer Before Sex" from Patheos.com)

GROW TOWARD FORGIVENESS

By the time women reach midlife, we've experienced all kinds of things in our relationships, some good, some bad. It's great to think back on the positive experiences once in a while, maybe even re-live them from time to time.

For the negative experiences, that's not such a good idea.

And the more serious the situation, the harder it is to not think about it. Maybe you've had to deal with an infidelity or some other kind of betrayal by your partner. If so, its lingering effects may very well be interfering with your ability to fully embrace your partner in a healthy–and even in a literal–way.

If you're harboring resentment or anger over some past wrong, you need to address it. As psychotherapist and our relationship coach Mary Jo Rapini says, "When your relationship struggles with resentment, it can feel like you are sleeping with the enemy. The resentment is felt deeply by one of the partners, and although it is rarely discussed openly, the tension can be felt by anyone close to the couple."

Let me be clear that I'm not talking about ignoring or deferring your feelings about a current situation in which you are being harmed or threatened. Rather, this is about that old wound that is getting in the way for you and your partner.

So how do you let go of it? That process is what we usually call forgiveness. Dr. Fred Luskin, a psychologist affiliated with Stanford

University, has made the study of forgiveness his life's work; he's written several books on it. The first, Forgive for Good, is based on the successful workshops he conducts using a step-by-step process to teach people how to forgive.

His second book, Forgive for Love, was written specifically for husbands and wives, and came about, he explains, because so many of his workshop participants were women trying to forgive current or ex-husbands.

Dr. Luskin has done studies that show harboring feelings of resentment and anger is not good for us physically or emotionally. It means we're in a constant state of stress and negativity. In lectures he often quotes Nelson Mandela: "Harboring resentment is like drinking poison to kill your enemy." In other words, it's doing a lot more harm to you than it is to the person who hurt you.

His methods of letting go of anger are similar to stress management and include mind-over-matter techniques like visualization and focusing on positive thoughts rather than negative ones.

Mary Jo, too, advises readers who are angry to "make a peace with your past. If it's possible in your circumstances, tell whoever hurt you how you feel about what happened." She also says that "letting go of your ego and learning to forgive your partner for their flaws and weaknesses—as well as forgiving yourself for holding on to that anger—are two of the biggest obstacles to overcome when working through resentment."

Learning to forgive may not be easy, but it's worth a try. In fact, it can be a life-changing experience. Because it's never too late to take action. And you'll feel much better when you do.

SEX THERAPY: NOT SO SCARY AFTER ALL!

The idea of going to a sex therapist may be so scary that you wouldn't even consider it! You're probably not alone. That's why we decided to talk with Sarah Young, MA, who is a sexual therapy specialist whose practice is Christian-based.

Chapter Two: Intention and Intimacy

Sarah was educated at the Institute for Sexual Wholeness in Atlanta; her philosophy is that sex is not just sacred, it's meant to be enjoyed. "It's still such a taboo issue," she says. Her goal is to help people find a "voice" for their sex lives, to talk about it and explore it freely without shame or guilt.

Q: What's the biggest "fear factor" or misconception women have about sex therapy?

A: Sex is such a personal, intimate thing. They're afraid they're going to have to get naked and perform: Oh, my gosh, am I going to have to take my clothes off and show her what we do? That's not how it works at all.

Q: Let's talk about how it does work: How do you get started?

A: A lot of my referrals come from doctors working with women, so I'll usually start with the woman. We'll just have a conversation at first. Patients often ask how I got into sex therapy, and that gives me the opportunity to establish my professionalism, my ethics, and how I feel about the sacredness of sex, which always makes them feel more comfortable.

Then we'll begin by talking about the bigger picture, her world as a whole: What are her other life stressors? I need to get an idea of everything that's going on in her life, the larger dynamic, because it's all entwined in the bigger circle. It's not a simple matter of just getting immediate details.

Facing failure goes against what Hollywood says your sex life should be; it's very threatening for people. So I try to validate her in that first session—here's where you are and this is fine—and to offer her hope.

Then in the second session, I'll usually engage in a pretty in-depth sexual history just to find out where she's coming from. What are her automatic thoughts, how has her body image been formed, and what other experiences are in her reality? Some of the questions are very difficult for people, like whether she is masturbating, and if so, how often.

Once we uncover all the issues, we'll talk about a game plan. At that point, I usually give it three weeks to a month between sessions, so they can just go through a cycle of life. Because you need to give this time; one week you might have a hormone issue, the next week, everything is okay. You need that whole cycle to give it a framework.

Q: What kinds of issues do you typically deal with in older women?

A: One big thing, of course, is menopause and all the changes that come with it. Women sometimes feel defective when they're going through it, which is understandable. Often it's a matter of shifting their perspective to just normalizing it; it is what it is, you need to take it one chunk at a time.

Other issues might be aging in general, or a partner's infidelity, or the reality of cancer and mastectomies: How am I still supposed to feel sexy when my breasts are gone? And the empty nesters: The kids have gone off and mom and dad haven't paid attention to each other for years. Now all of a sudden, she's thinking, I don't even know how to be his friend, let alone his lover. So a lot of it is empowering people to reignite the passion and the friendship they once had; they're in a place when they can engage in a more mature perspective.

Q: Once a person starts therapy, how long might it last?

A: It really depends... I have couples I'll see every few weeks for three months and they'll check in after that every few months to update, or if they've hit a glitch or want to talk through it. Every case is different, really.

Q: At what point does the woman's partner usually get involved?

A: Usually, I work with a woman for about a month before bringing in her partner. At that point, I try to get a feel for where he's coming from, whether he wants to meet individually. If he does, we might move ahead where every other session is with the couple–so it's couple, individual, couple, individual, through the duration of the therapy.

Q: What are some of the therapy techniques you use with couples?

A: We have many techniques, but if we need to talk about the basics, such as specific sexual positions and so on, I have these two little pipe cleaner people. The little blue person with the erection represents the man, and the pink one, with little boobs, is the woman. It's delightful because some people have a problem even looking at pictures, so it's a very neutral way to teach people positions.

I'll also suggest readings, and we use a lot of sensate focus, too, which is kind of the default "go-to" for sex therapy in terms of reintroducing touch to couples. They rediscover the joy of just looking at each other, or sitting together, or holding each other. That also gives the therapist some control to say, okay, I'm going to take over your sex lives for awhile. You don't have to worry about whether you should be doing this or doing that. You just have to do this one exercise, and it's not even going to involve your genitals.

Because sex is not just about orgasms; it's not just about his erect penis and your lubricated vagina. If that's how it's framed for couples, they're doomed for failure. But if they can broaden their definition of the sexual experience, it's huge for them in terms of being allies in the bedroom, on the same team, saying, this stage of life can be fabulous, how can we really embrace it?

Q: Can you give an example of a successful case involving a husband and wife?

A: There was a woman who came to see me because she wasn't enjoying sex; for her entire married life it had been, "Okay, let's just get this over with…" Come to find out, when she was a little girl, she was experimenting with masturbation, as kids often do. Her mother, who was very uptight about sex, discovered her and flipped out, making her filled with shame and guilt over it.

First we had to deal with her wounds, dissolving some of the lies she believed and getting her to see her sexuality from an adult perspective, rather than through the eyes of a seven-year-old. We talked about how a person's sexuality is not just limited to the bedroom; it's part of who you are every day. I gave her some exercises to increase her confidence. For instance, a lot of women will look in the mirror and just see sagging boobs and cellulite. But I had her stand in front of the mirror and take joy in her hands, the hands that had held her children and made food for her family. And instead of keeping her sex drive on a low boil, I told her to go get some red underwear to remind herself that she's a beautiful, sexual woman who has a right to enjoy and to be enjoyed by her husband. So it was getting her to see things in a new way, as an adult.

Over a period of time, she began to gain confidence, becoming more mentally present with him in the bedroom. And it just kind of took off from there. She's still working on not feeling uptight, but she's doing really great.

Q: *Your work must be very satisfying. Do you enjoy it?*

A: I absolutely love it; to see the hope in a woman's eyes when she finds out she's not crazy or abnormal or to see a husband who feels like he's got his wife back, it's just the best thing.

QUESTIONS... AND ANSWERS

Q: Is emotional intimacy necessary to good sex?

Let's first acknowledge that women—and men, too—come to sex with a host of different backgrounds, value sets, cultural expectations, emotional foundations, and experiences. It's very difficult, given that variety, to assert that anything is or should be true for every woman.

It is theoretically possible to have a strong physical attraction and enjoy sex with little emotional intimacy involved—whether we are men or women. There are differences between us, though: Research suggests that for women there are six neurotransmitters involved in sexual activity, and that the areas that "light up" in our brains with sex are completely different from men's responses. Women release oxytocin with sex, a very strong bonding hormone; men don't.

Cultural stereotypes may exaggerate the differences between men and women when it comes to sex, but the science is there to prove there are differences.

Among the women in my practice and in the rest of life, I observe that women often go into sexual experiences with an expected outcome that includes some emotional connection. Most of the women I see desire emotional intimacy as a cornerstone for their enjoyment of physical intimacy. And the study I recall that went the furthest in qualifying sexual enjoyment (see the last section of this book) implied emotional intimacy as intertwined with physical intimacy.

All of that said, I come back to the fact that women come to sex with enormous variety of experience and expectation. As long as she is caring for her own emotional and physical safety and health, each woman can choose, I hope, the right combination of emotional and physical intimacy.

Q: Am I stuck with an unfulfilling sex life?

No! It's great that you recognize the value of remaining sexually active, despite your decreasing libido.

As we get older, we have to learn some new techniques to continue to enjoy sex. You can use this book or the MiddlesexMD website to have a discussion with your husband: Either will help him understand what you're experiencing, and that it's not "about him." Review together the bonding behaviors and alternatives to intercourse.

You may find a role for erotica, like DVDs or books. Just this week a woman told me that she keeps a book of erotica nearby. It works really well for her to read from it in anticipation of sex (although her husband isn't aware she has it for this purpose).

If you're comfortable with the idea, incorporating a vibrator may help; after menopause we do require more stimulation for arousal and orgasm.

Healthy relationships require intimacy—it's worth the effort.

Q: Should I worry if I found an erotic video arousing?

Absolutely not! As we grow older, it takes more stimulation for us to arouse and lubricate, and that stimulation can come in many forms–physical or mental. If watching an erotic video provided visual stimulation for you… well, you're not alone!

It's sometimes a challenge to find the right material–arousing but not offensive–but it sounds like you found it! Don't feel guilty or embarrassed. Most women need to change things up a bit and adding erotica is a perfectly acceptable option.

Q: How can I feel intimate with an emotionally remote husband?

I posed this question to Mary Jo Rapini, an advisor to MiddlesexMD and a therapist, writer, and speaker. Here's her advice:

You're not alone in your feelings of being married to a man who cannot express his love. I am happy that you are healthy enough to advocate for yourself and your own sexual and emotional needs. There are several things I can suggest that may really help you feel more connected to your husband—and will help you feel better as well.

The SmartMarriages website has good information that can help you and your husband. They are very pro marriage, but more than that, they are pro relationship. Anyone who wants to improve her relationship could benefit from their resources.

Read a book called The Five Love Languages, by Gary Chapman. Many couples have found it helpful; men like it, too, and reading it together will lead to better understanding of each other and how you each feel most loved. The author also offers weekend classes throughout the U.S.; you might find him in your area.

You and your husband would benefit from attending a marital retreat. If he doesn't like groups, or if you don't, I would suggest a private therapist. I think your husband would feel less threatened if you sought out a male therapist.

One of the most beneficial experiences to help couples become more emotional in their loving and more connected is attending Tantric classes, offered in many cities. They are a bit unusual, and some guys (especially older) are reluctant to attend, but if you can persuade him to go to just one, he will enjoy it.

Remember that men are raised to be competitive. They usually open up to their wives, but fear being "too vulnerable." This may generalize to their sexuality. Try more touching with him and less talking or trying to "process emotions."

Make sure you're taking care of yourself, including having someone you can talk to! You need emotional support so you can regain your strength and confidence.

CHAPTER THREE

PLAYING IT SAFE

SO OVER CONTRACEPTION?

Think Again.

Yeah, I know. You've been doing the contraception shuffle for, oh, decades now. Isn't it "safe" yet? After all, you're past 40. Maybe you've even missed a couple periods.

Not so fast.

You're in the midst of a very hazardous crossing—those uncertain years between fertility and menopause during which you are less likely to get pregnant, but, make no mistake, you still can!

While women are indeed less fertile after 40, they absolutely can get pregnant. In fact, women can conceive even during perimenopause, when the menstrual cycle is beginning to become irregular.

For some reason, however, women seem to become more casual as they near the goalposts. How else to account for the fact that women over 40 are the least likely to use birth control of any age group, and that their abortion rates are as high as those of adolescents, according to a 2008 *USA Today* article.

In Great Britain, women in their 40s are now called "the Sex and the City generation," and they, too, have grown careless. In the UK,

Chapter Three: Playing it Safe

abortions within the over-40 age group have risen by one-third in the past decade. In the US, 38 percent of pregnancies in women age 40 and older are unplanned. Of those, 56 percent end in abortion, according to an article in HealthyWomen.org.

By the time they reach 40, women are generally old hands at birth control. But at this point in life some reevaluation may be in order. Levels of fertility are decreasing, and hormonal levels are (or soon will be) in flux. Some women may not want to have children; others may want to keep the option open. In any case, an unplanned surprise complicates life really fast.

This is a good time for a conversation about birth control with your health care provider, and you may have to initiate it. While you have more options than ever, the best one for you might be different than what worked for you in your 20s.

And just so you know, current guidelines advise that you remain on birth control until *one year after* your last period, the official definition of menopause. Complicating the picture is the fact that with hormonal forms of birth control, such as the pill, your cycles may be irregular or may stop completely, which masks the onset of menopause. And the withdrawal bleed during the week off the pill isn't considered a true period.

Birth control after 40 falls into several categories: permanent, long-term or short, hormonal or barrier method. They vary in levels of effectiveness and in the side effects you may experience. And remember that condoms are the only type of birth control that protects against sexually transmitted infections.

Probably your most immediate decision is whether to end childbearing permanently. Tubal ligation is a laparoscopic procedure that happens under general anesthetic in a hospital. There's also a newer, minimally invasive surgical option that a doctor can do with a local anesthetic right in the office. Or, of course, your partner could have permanent sterilization as an outpatient office procedure.

Hormonal types of birth control are very effective, but can have both side effects (bloating, mood disruption, risk of stroke for some women) as well as protective benefits (against bone loss and some forms of cancer, for example). It is very important to carefully review your health history with your health care provider to select the best option for you.

Short-term hormonal options include

- » Combined estrogen-progestogen pill (COCP). This is "the pill" you are probably familiar with. Since it now has very low estrogen levels, it's considered safe for women who have no risk factors until age 55.

- » Progestogen-only pill (POP), which is a good option for older women. It must be taken regularly at the same time of day, however.

- » A patch, which also releases low dosages of estrogen and progestogen.

- » Vaginal rings release low dosages of estrogen. The ring is kept in the vagina for three weeks, then removed for a week.

Long-term hormonal options include

- » Progestogen shot, which is a once-every-8-12-week option.

- » Progestogen implant, in which a tiny rod is inserted in the upper arm. It lasts for three years.

- » An IUD impregnated with progestogen, which is highly effective and lasts for years.

The old non-hormonal standbys still include

- » Condom. Again, the only birth control that also protects against STIs.

- » Non-hormonal IUD. Also highly effective and long-lasting.

- » Diaphragm with spermicide, cervical cap, or spermicidal sponge.

Your choice of birth control at this point should be informed and careful. You need a plan to carry you through menopause, and you need to begin the dialog with your health care provider.

Since the consequences of ignoring the issue are so life-changing, this conversation ought to begin now!

STIS–NOT JUST YOUR DAUGHTER'S (OR GRANDDAUGHTER'S) CONCERN

She's 54 years old. She's spent most of her adult life in a long-term monogamous relationship. She's just been diagnosed with genital herpes.

This happens more often than you might think.

Even I—who should know better!—have been guilty of age bias when it comes to testing for sexually transmitted infections (STIs, also called STDs, for sexually transmitted diseases).

In my former practice, when a 20-year-old came in presenting with symptoms (discharge, discomfort, irritation) that might indicate an STI, I would automatically screen her. When a 50- or 60-year-old came to me with the same symptoms, I was more likely to ask before I tested: "Is this a possibility?" If she said "no," I tended to trust that. I was trusting my patients. They were trusting their partners.

Times have changed.

Over the past decade, STI rates among people 45 and older more than doubled. In April 2010, the Centers for Disease Control and Prevention reported that senior citizens accounted for 24 percent of total AIDS cases, up from 17 percent in 2001.

Researchers point to climbing divorce rates at midlife, the rise of online dating services, the increasing number of men availing themselves of treatment for erectile dysfunction. And all of these are contributing factors, I'm sure. But in my experience, the most likely cause of the up-tick in STIs among women past their childbearing years is lack of awareness and prevention.

If you know that pregnancy is not a possibility, why use a condom?

Unfortunately, the risk of contracting STIs—including syphilis, gonorrhea, genital herpes, HPV, hepatitis B, and HIV—does not end at menopause. In fact, sexually active postmenopausal women may be more vulnerable than younger women; the thinning, more delicate genital tissue that comes with age is also more prone to small cuts or tears that provide pathways for infection.

And—it's not fair, but there it is—with almost every STI, exposed men are less likely to experience symptoms, simply because they don't have the equivalent of a cervix and a vagina and the skin of a vulva. The kind, older gentleman who gave my 54-year-old patient genital herpes might honestly not have known he was infected.

These days, when a 50-or-60-ish woman shows up in my office with symptoms that point to a possible STI, I go ahead and screen. I'll say, "I understand this is not a likely outcome, but I want to make sure I'm checking all possibilities."

Worry about STI can be a real drag on sexual enjoyment. Keep reading to see what you can do to ensure that contracting an STI is not a possibility for you.

WHEN WAS THE LAST TIME YOU USED A CONDOM?

It's a personal question, I know, but one I'm trying to be sure to ask my midlife and older patients who are newly single and sexually active.

Among women our age, sexually transmitted infections (STIs) are up and condom use is down. There's a direct correlation.

Those of us who have spent the last 30 to 40 years in long-term monogamous relationships may not have even seen a condom in that time, let alone bought and used one. When contraception was the goal

Chapter Three: Playing it Safe

and a steady partner was the norm, we tended to choose less intrusive methods of protection–like the pill or IUDs.

Now, though, if you're single and entertaining the possibility of a new sexual relationship, it's time to get acquainted or reacquainted with the most effective means of preventing transmission of STIs like gonorrhea, HPV, herpes, chlamydia, and HIV: the venerable condom. Because it's an actual physical barrier, and because it's the easiest barrier to use, it's the most effective option we've seen.

Of course you can buy condoms at your local drugstore or grocery store, but if you don't want your kid's best friend waiting on you, you may want to consider an online source. And if you've never bought or used latex protection before, don't worry. Our website offers basic instructions for using condoms.

(A parenthetical note: We know there are female condoms, which work just fine as a barrier for protection. But when we actually tested them as part of our product selection, we found them too clunky for us to be comfortable. We wouldn't recommend them to our friends. But we'll keep an eye on the options and let you know when something better comes along–or let us know if you've found a brand or a method that makes them your preference.)

A few more tips to help build your condom confidence:

» Keep a ready supply on hand–in a zippered pocket of your purse, in a drawer of your nightstand, or some other nifty bedside storage. Scrambling around for that little packet in the heat of passion can cool things down in a hurry.

» Talk with your partner about condom use as soon as it seems clear that sexual intimacy is a definite possibility for the two of you. Agreeing that protection is essential–and deciding who's in charge of making sure it's there when the time is right–will ease anxiety and embarrassment for both of you.

» Incorporate condoms into your sex play and lovemaking. Application can be quite exciting in itself!

Finally, remember that not even your friendly condom offers 100-percent protection. In addition to insisting on a latex condom, NAMS (North American Menopause Society) guidelines for safer sex include choosing partners wisely and discussing sexual histories, getting an annual exam that includes testing for STIs, and making sure that your Hepatitis B vaccine is up to date.

The Virus that Doesn't Go Away

There are literally millions of women in the U.S. who have the genital herpes virus—including many of us at midlife. Not everyone is aware that outbreaks can increase during menopause, which concerns not only women who've managed the virus within a relationship, but also those who may be considering a new relationship.

The most obvious reason for the increase in occurrences is that menopause may cause some stresses; as you probably know if you carry the virus, stress can trigger outbreaks. Also, aging makes genital tissue more delicate and prone to small cuts or tears that provide pathways for infection. Many more of us are single at this stage of life these days; if we're sexually active with multiple partners, that can increase the rate of infection overall in our age group.

(By the way, herpes and other sexually transmitted infections are most commonly transmitted from men to women, but they can pass from woman to woman as well.)

Nothing yet makes genital herpes go away permanently. Symptoms can be controlled with medication, either taken daily to minimize the number of outbreaks or at the onset of an outbreak to limit its duration or intensity. If you're currently taking meds, there's no reason not to continue during menopause, even if you're on hormones. If your medicine isn't as effective as it was, talk to your doctor about upping the dosage or switching to another. If you're experiencing more frequent outbreaks, you may want to consider the continuous daily approach.

Whether you're single and contemplating intimacy or in a long-term relationship, there are some things you can do to avoid sharing this virus with your partner:

» Avoid sexual contact from the moment the symptoms first appear until the sores have completely healed.

» Don't let embarrassment stop you from discussing your sexual history; it's imperative that your partner be aware of your situation. (And vice-versa!)

» Prevent transfer of any bodily fluids to cuts or other openings.

» Use a condom for any kind of sex–oral, genital or anal.

» Keep fit and have regular physicals.

» Keep the infected area clean and dry.

» Don't touch the sores. If you do have contact, wash your hands right away.

I'm happy to report, too, that researchers are vigorously exploring ways to protect women from the herpes virus and prevent it from spreading. One solution might be a herpes vaccine; other possibilities include gels and creams that could kill the virus before it has the chance to infect someone else.

But until scientists do come up with a more effective way to fight herpes, stay on your meds, manage your stress, be mindful, and stay healthy!

QUESTIONS... AND ANSWERS

Q: If my partner previously had a partner with HPV, am I at risk?

HPV (Human Papilloma Virus) is so common that the lifetime cumulative risk of being an HPV carrier is 80 percent. In other words, we're nearly all carriers of HPV.

Fortunately, most people do not suffer adverse effects. Reactions to HPV exposure depends on our immune systems and whether we are exposed to high-risk or low-risk HPV types. The most common consequences for women are vulvar warts or abnormal pap smears, but, again, most women have no symptoms at all.

So you can assume two things: That your partner (like 80 percent of adults) is an HPV carrier, but that the likelihood of a health consequence is small. If this proves to be a long-term relationship, enjoying sex without a condom will be acceptable and safe for you.

For anyone entering into a new relationship: Getting screened for sexually transmitted infections is smart–and it's a way of signaling you care about each other and the new beginning you're making together.

Q: Can I be re-infected with HPV by my husband of 20 years?

It's estimated that up to 80 percent of all adults have come in contact with HPV and are therefore carriers. Any HPV that you or he introduced to the relationship 20 years ago, you were both exposed to initially—and remember, we basically all bring HPV into every relationship! If you have been in the same, monogamous relationship for 20 years, you cannot be 're-infected' by the same HPV type. There's no need for concern–or for condoms or other preventive measures!

There are over 100 different subtypes of HPV. Fortunately, nearly all are 'low risk,' and only a few are 'high risk.' The low-risk types are now felt to be mostly an inconvenience without any true long-term risk. The few high-risk types (e.g., type 16, 18, 35) have a risk of causing progressive cellular changes, putting a woman at risk for cervical cancer.

Relax and enjoy sex without a condom within your relationship! (Just remember, if over time you do have a new partner, you can expose

Chapter Three: Playing it Safe

him to the HPV type that you carry. A condom will reduce the risk of exposure).

Q: What's the connection between abnormal pap results and HPV?

HPV is the most common cause of abnormal pap smears.

It is only fairly recently that we get more specific results with pap smears, telling us whether an 'abnormal' finding is related to a low-risk or high-risk HPV type. If it's low-risk, we are likely to treat it like a normal pap smear, with a follow up recommended based on the specifics of your findings and history. High-risk HPV requires further follow-up, typically a colposcopy and possibly a biopsy. (Don't be alarmed by "colposcopy," by the way. I know it's a scary word, but it only means using a bright light and magnification to inspect the cervix.) Pap smear guidelines have changed significantly in the past 3 years because we understand much more about the behavior of the viruses now.

These more advanced pap smears, by telling us more about the HPV, save many women the inconvenience, cost, and discomfort of those further tests.

We're not sure why women develop an abnormal pap smear 10 to 15 years after an initial exposure to an HPV type. It probably has to do with the viral type of HPV (remember most are low risk), your immune system, and other factors we don't know. A new 'abnormal' pap smear result is not evidence that you have been re-infected. If you have been with the same partner, had an occasional abnormal pap, but nothing has progressed significantly, you are unlikely to have an aggressive, high-risk HPV type.

Q: What non-hormonal birth control can I use when I go off the pill?

There are two principle non-surgical options for birth control: hormonal and barrier methods. Sounds like you've already decided to steer clear of hormones, at least for a time.

The most common barrier options include condoms (male or female) or diaphragms, in combination with a vaginal spermicide. (Vaginal spermicides, available as film, foam, and suppositories, have a slightly higher failure rate than other methods when used alone.) We haven't yet found a female condom that is easy to use and reliable–let us know if you have a recommendation! Don't count on condoms that have been rattling around in a drawer while you've been on the pill: Freshness does count so the condoms aren't brittle.

You'll need to talk to your health care provider about a diaphragm, since it needs to fit you well.

And, of course, there are surgical options for your partner (vasectomy) or for you (tubal interruption). Again, a discussion with your health care provider will help you weigh those options.

You're smart to be thinking ahead about this!

CHAPTER FOUR

GETTING COMFORTABLE

Because lower estrogen levels affect the natural vaginal lubricant that made life so simple when we were younger, we may need lubricants or vaginal moisturizers to keep our vaginal tissues in shape and responsive.

WE SHALL OVERCOME: DRYNESS

Itchy beyond words. Crotch of underwear rubs painfully against labia. Sensation of being on the receiving end of a vulvar wedgie. Feels like tiny razor blade nicks in my vagina during intercourse without lube or adequate foreplay. Also difficulty with penetration.

Doesn't that sound awful? If that were you, I wouldn't be surprised that you're not thinking about sex. Just as awful, about half of us think that vaginal dryness is something we just have to live with—and about the same number of us are hesitant to raise the topic with our doctors.

The truth is that vaginal dryness does not need to end the intimacy you have with your partner—or the afterglow you experience yourself after sex.

First, a word about what's happening: Yes, it's likely hormones. As estrogen levels decline, the vaginal lining changes. It becomes more delicate and less stretchy. There's less lubrication and less circulation. Vaginal dryness is a typical first sign of vaginal atrophy, when vulvo-vaginal tissues shorten and tighten. It's common; you're not alone, and you're not deficient.

If you're just beginning to notice some discomfort, you can take the easy step of adding lubricant to your foreplay. Lubricants come in three types: water-based, silicone, and hybrid. My patients with dryness issues typically like the silicone and hybrid best, because they last the longest without reapplication, and because they seem just a little bit slipperier to some. Lubricants are made specifically for safe use on and in your vagina; you may want to experiment with a few, because they do have different scents and textures.

Next, you can add a vaginal moisturizer. While lubricants provide temporary comfort, reducing friction during sex, moisturizers work to "feed" and strengthen vaginal tissues around the clock. Moisturizing here is just like moisturizing your neck or your face: You have to be faithful! I recommend application at least twice a week. Moisturizers need to be placed directly in your vagina, which can be done with an applicator or a clean syringe you reserve for that purpose.

For some women, these two products—and the right amount of foreplay—are enough to make a difference. If they don't do it for you, please talk to your health care provider, even if you think it will be awkward: Your sex life is important! There are localized estrogen products and a relatively new oral medication (called Osphena) that may be helpful for you, but you'll need a consultation with your physician and a prescription.

This isn't the end; it's only a transition, which we as women have a lot of practice with. Take heart and take charge!

MOIST IS GOOD

In the last chapter, we talked about how pH levels affect the vagina. The second part of good vaginal health has to do with moisture. As we say at MiddlesexMD, moist tissues are strong tissues.

Normally, your vagina moisturizes and cleanses itself by secreting a clear fluid that seeps from blood vessels in the vaginal wall. When

Chapter Four: Getting Comfortable

you become sexually aroused, blood flow increases, and so does the lubrication. Unfortunately, this process is regulated by estrogen, and we all know what's been happening to that hormone lately.

With decreasing estrogen levels and circulation, vaginal tissue becomes thin and dry. Maybe you've noticed that you don't lubricate as easily during sex so that penetration is difficult or painful, or maybe you've experienced vaginal dryness and discomfort at other times as well.

The good news is that this condition is easy to fix. You moisturize your skin regularly; you should do the same with the vagina.

First, a little refresher on the difference between vaginal moisturizers and lubricants. Lubricants may be used in the vagina and on the penis or toys during intercourse to help with penetration and to make sex more pleasurable. Lubricants come in water- or silicone-based varieties or a hybrid of the two, and in various viscosities (thick to thin). Choice of lubricant is a highly personal preference and may depend on the activity you have in mind.

Lubricants last up to several hours, and the only rule of thumb related to vaginal health is that no oil-based product, including petroleum jelly, should be used in the vagina. They're hard for the vagina to flush out; they tend to disrupt pH balance; they may promote infections for some; and they also tend to deteriorate condoms. Lubricants can be used in addition to a moisturizer.

The sole purpose of vaginal moisturizers, on the other hand, is to keep vaginal tissue moist and healthy. Moisturizers last two or three days and should be used regularly, just like facial products. And just like anything you use on your body, you want your vaginal moisturizer to contain natural, high-quality ingredients.

A few common ingredients in vaginal moisturizers (that are also present in lubricants) bear some examination:

» Glycerin. Widely used in moisturizers and lubricants, glycerin is a colorless, sweet-tasting substance that can exacerbate a yeast infection by giving the organisms sugars to feed on. If you're susceptible to yeast infections, find a glycerin-free moisturizer.

» Parabens. In all their hyphenated mutations (methyl-, ethyl-, butyl, and propyl-) parabens are a widely used preservative and antimicrobial agent. While some contamination-fighting ingredient is a good idea in these personal products, a few recent studies have found very slight health issues that may be linked to parabens. A bigger problem is the potential for an allergic reaction that could be related to parabens or other ingredients in moisturizers.

» Propylene glycol. Used as a fragrance and to control viscosity, propylene glycol has also been linked to skin irritations and allergies.

While none of these substances present major health risks, it's a good idea to make an informed decision about your personal care products. Read the ingredient list in your moisturizer; the fewer unpronounceable names, the better. If you can find a product that uses natural ingredients and that works for you, wouldn't that be your first choice?

VAGINAL HEALTH BEGINS WITH BUGS

When you think about it, the vagina is a pretty undemanding organ. It's cooperated through childbirth and nights of passion; it's soldiered on uncomplainingly throughout years of menses and the occasional "oops"—such as the patient of mine who applied Retin-A skin cream instead of Vagisil, or the friend who used Ben-Gay. Her vagina did a little complaining then, but soon returned to its cheerful self.

Because the vagina has rarely been the squeaky wheel, we've tended to take it for granted. As we age, however, vaginal tissue thins, loses elasticity, and becomes dry, so, like other parts of our bodies, that wheel tends to squeak a little louder.

Often, vaginal troubles can be addressed—or avoided altogether—with some TLC. While few of us think about how to maintain optimal vaginal health, maybe it's time to give that long-suffering organ some extra attention. The two major factors in maintaining a healthy, uncomplaining vagina are a good bacterial balance and moisture.

First, a science lesson: pH is a measure of how acidic or alkaline (basic) a substance is. The pH scale ranges from 0 (very acidic) to 14 (highly alkaline) with seven being neutral. A healthy vagina is slightly acidic, in the range of 3.5 to 5. This acidity is maintained by a delicate balance of organisms, notably the bacteria lactobacillus that produces lactic acid. This slightly acid environment helps to ward off infection.

When the pH level in our vagina is out of whack, unwanted bacteria and other organisms can flourish—Candida albicans, for example, which is the fungus causing yeast infections. Sometimes it doesn't take much to upset the balance. A sugary diet, some kinds of soap, a round of antibiotics, or even one of those nights of passion can upset the flora in the vagina. Sperm, for example, is alkaline with a pH of 7 to 8, and so is blood with a pH of 7.4, which is why hygiene is especially important if you're still menstruating.

Here are some suggestions for maintaining a good pH balance and for overall vaginal hygiene.

» Don't douche. Douching actually increases the risk of bacterial infection and reduces the "good" lactobacilli in the vagina. The vaginal walls produce a clear fluid to flush out foreign substances (more on this in the next post), so douching is both unnecessary and harmful.

» Maintain good air flow. Wear cotton panties and loose clothing—at least some of the time! Avoid relying on silks and synthetics that trap moisture on the vulva. Change out of wet bathing suits or clothing promptly.

» Avoid scented products: feminine sprays, soaps, bubble bath, scented pads or tampons. They can be irritating, allergenic, or alkaline.

» Wash your bottom with warm water. Soap is drying to the delicate vulva and inner labia, and some soaps are alkaline.

» Use tampons rather than pads and change them regularly.

» Keep bacteria where they belong. Wipe from front to rear.

» Avoid sugars and refined carbohydrates. They can create an environment that feeds fungi.

» Talk to your doctor about maintaining good vaginal health if you're prescribed antibiotics.

» Wash underwear with mild soap, such as Woolite. Rinse well. Avoid scented fabric softeners.

At the end of the day, all our parts are interconnected, so it's not possible to maintain good vaginal health if the rest of your body is unhealthy. Smoking, obesity, and diabetes are all conditions that compromise health, including vaginal health. Good general habits, such as a healthy diet and exercise to maintain good muscle tone, are probably the most critical elements to a healthy vagina.

But you knew that.

"NOTHING TO BE DONE ABOUT PAIN?" NOT SO.

There's another topic that many women aren't talking about, even though lots of women experience it. It's painful intercourse.

In the REVEAL research study, 36 percent of women said that pain during sex made them stop having sex. That's one issue. The other issue is that 59 percent of women who experience pain during sex still have intercourse on a regular basis. About three-quarters of those women have sex at least once a month, on average; a third have sex at least once a week.

The good news for the women among the 59 percent is that they recognize their sexuality as an important part of their selves and their relationships. The bad news, of course, is that it hurts. And more bad news is that not enough women realize that it doesn't have to.

When midlife women talk about their sexuality, pain with sex is easily the most common physical complaint. This pain may feel superficial or deep. It may feel like burning or aching. It may happen only on initial penetration or only with deep thrusting.

The medical name for this is *dyspareunia* (dis-pu-ROO-nee-uh). It's a tongue twister of a word, I know, but it comes from "dys" (as in dysfunctional) plus a Greek word that means "lying with"—so it's as simple as "lying together doesn't work." It's a general diagnosis that needs more investigation, because many things can cause the pain, and the pain can be experienced in a number of ways.

Another scary part of the research: A quarter of the women who experience painful intercourse thought that there was "nothing that could be done medically" to address their pain; I assure you that's not true. There are solutions ranging from regular use of moisturizers and personal lubricants to overcome dryness to vaginal dilators to restore vaginal caliber (size and depth of the opening) to systemic or vaginal estrogen to maintain tissue health.

About a quarter also felt that their pain during sex was "an inappropriate conversation" to have with their health care provider; that's not true, either.

Easy for me to say, I know, since I specialize in midlife women's health. Whoever your health care provider is, he or she will recognize the importance of sexuality to a full and healthy life. And if you don't sense that, it's worth it to find a sexually literate health care provider. Really.

PAIN DURING SEX? ESCAPE THE CYCLE

Vaginismus, a vaginal muscle spasm that prevents penetration, can be part of a vicious cycle of pain and response. If you experience painful intercourse, your natural desire to avoid the pain may be a psychological trigger for vaginismus, which occurs involuntarily.

How do you know whether it's time to talk to your doctor? The keys are frequency and persistence, but I hate to tell women they need to endure pain for any specific length of time before they talk to me about it. If pain is recurring or persistent, if you take note of it, if it affects your ability to enjoy intimacy, I'd recommend that you talk to your health care practitioner.

Maybe you've been avoiding going to the doctor because you're afraid the exam will be painful, and that's very understandable. And you're not alone, believe me! Pelvic exams cause anxiety in most women—even without the added complication of suspected vaginismus. But a trusted gynecologist or menopause practitioner will be very familiar with vaginismus and related conditions and will know how to approach the exam.

If you're uncomfortable talking about what you're experiencing with your doctor, consider taking this book with you to get the discussion started. Write down your exact symptoms—where it hurts and when—so you can describe what's happening. You can also read more about vaginismus; learning about it will help you ask your doctor more specific questions, like, "Do my pelvic floor muscles seem too tight?"

Treatment requires the right combination of physical and cognitive therapies, especially if your condition is psychologically induced vaginismus. In that case, retraining the body and the mind to accept vaginal penetration is part of the treatment. Other techniques may include:

» The use of a dilator, which can increase your comfort gradually

» Botox injections

» Exercise, such as Kegel, and/or pelvic muscle therapy

» Pain management techniques

» Relaxation training

It's also worth noting that vaginismus is common among women who force themselves to have sex when sex is painful. I hope you're not one of them! If you are having pain during intercourse, please go to your doctor and let the healing begin. Then you—and your partner—can get back to enjoying sex again.

THE ULTIMATE COUPLE'S PROJECT: PAIN-FREE SEX

I'm still thinking about the research that says lots of post-menopause women have sex even though it hurts. The study I read said many of them think there's nothing that can be done—that painful sex is a normal part of being a mid-life woman.

I pick up clues to another obstacle in the emails I receive as Dr. Barb: We women are reluctant to include our partners in addressing difficulties with intercourse. I'm not sure why this is. Maybe we're in denial about the changes we're experiencing. Maybe we're too used to being the caretakers in our households. Maybe we're still shy about talking about our genitals and our pleasure.

If I overdo in the garden, my husband will give me a back rub. If a shipment of products for MiddlesexMD arrives after hours, he'll help me carry the heavier boxes in. When we entertain, we clear the clutter together.

I guess I'm suggesting that you see maintaining your sexuality as the ultimate couple's project. A partner who loves you will not want you to endure pain to give him pleasure; and will want you to enjoy intimacy as much as you are able.

You'll have to talk about it—as you'd tell him where the muscles are knotted after weeding. You can share this book or sit down with our website together to get the conversation moving.

He can plan to take more time to increase your arousal and natural lubrication. Together, you can use lubricant as part of foreplay to increase your comfort. The two of you can experiment with warming lubricants or a vibrator to increase your sensation. And your partner can support your work with dilators or other tools to regain your sexual health.

It's not too much to ask. Really.

VAGINAL PATENCY FOR SINGLE WOMEN

A lot of the patients in my menopause practice are single women. My patients who have no sexual partners can be quick to dismiss my questions about sexual symptoms, figuring that without a partner in their lives, they have no sexual concerns. I have two worries about that.

First, you don't need a partner to have orgasms. Self-satisfaction is good for us physically and mentally. As a doctor, I often encourage women to consider this, particularly older single women, because of the health benefits.

Second, self-stimulation helps us maintain patent vaginal tissues.

My friends would like me to point out that "patent" is a term doctors use when talking about tube-like structures. Patent means "open."

Maintaining patent vaginal tissues means making sure your vagina remains open, usable, in case one day you do find someone worthy of a sexual relationship.

If you have lived with your vagina for 40 years without giving it much of a thought, you should know that its patency has been maintained largely through hormonal influence. Now, as estrogen declines, particularly if it declines abruptly (as it does in surgical menopause), the tissues of your vagina will become thinner and more fragile, and circulation to those tissues will decrease.

If your vagina isn't receiving any stimulation, those changes will happen more quickly. The more you use your vagina, the slower the changes go. When we say "Use it or lose it," this is what we mean.

I have met plenty of patients who did not know that vaginas need to be maintained. When you can't see the vagina and have little use for it, it's easy to completely forget about it. Tissues became thin and dry, in more extreme cases the walls of the vagina adhere to one another, losing patency. In lay terms, vaginas begin to close up.

Chapter Four: Getting Comfortable

This can be very upsetting when love comes along later and we are faced with months of therapy to reopen and restore the vagina. It can be done, but it's so much easier to maintain patency than to lose it and then work to get it back. Often you can't completely restore what is lost.

What does it take to maintain patency? There are plenty of options ranging from localized estrogen therapy you can discuss with your doctor, or use of vaginal moisturizers, lubricants, and dilators. We also recommend regular clitoral stimulation, to maintain blood flow and keep your clitoris strong and responsive. And of course, Kegel exercises, which will not only help us maintain strong orgasms, but helps us retain urinary continence too.

We work hard after 40 to maintain our skin, our hair, our bodies, brains, and hearts. Why not our vulvovaginal tissues too? Strong vaginas are not just for couples!

KEEPING THINGS OPEN

Maybe you're divorced or widowed. Maybe you've been single and partnerless for a while. Maybe you found someone after a long dry spell. Or, maybe sex has just been darned painful lately.

Now, if you've been on the sidelines, sexually speaking, for a while, you won't be able to jump back into the game without some preparation. At this point, sex can be surprising, and not in a good way. With the loss of estrogen you've been experiencing lately, and especially if you haven't used it lately, your vagina actually begins to shrink and shorten.

Whether or not you're in a relationship, the name of the game remains "use it or lose it." And it's a lot easier to maintain vaginal health than to play catch-up after ignoring the situation downtown for a while.

What specifically can you do? We've talked about moisturizers, practicing your kegels, using a vibrator or other form of self-pleasuring as part of your sexual health maintenance program.

But another important tool, especially if you're currently without a partner (or are trying to rehabilitate now that you've found someone) is the regular use of dilators.

Say what?

Dilators are sets of tubes, usually made of high-quality, cleanable plastic or silicone that start small (half-inch) and gradually larger (up to an inch and a half). They're inserted into the vagina in gradually increasing sizes to stretch the vaginal walls, making them open enough (which is called patency) and capacious enough to do their job.

It isn't quick, but it is effective.

Occasionally, I run across suggestions for homemade dilators that make use of various round objects. Don't try this. It's important for all kinds of reasons to use only high-quality dilators that are smooth and easy to hold, that increase in size gradually and consistently, and that can be cleaned well.

You should only use the safest, highest quality product in this important place. If you don't know where to look, we offer a selection of dilators on our website that we've carefully vetted.

These will work much better for you than those candles you were eyeing.

Here's how you use them:

RELAX. Take a bath—it makes all those tissues soft and pliable. Lie comfortably on your back with your knees open.

LUBRICATE the smallest dilator well with a vaginal lubricant.

GENTLY INSERT it into the vagina. Keep all those pelvic floor muscles relaxed. Breathe. Push the dilator in as far as you comfortably can.

HOLD it there for 20 to 30 minutes. Do this twice a day.

When you can comfortably insert the smallest dilator, graduate to the next largest size.

It can take three months or more to restore vaginal capacity. Once you're comfortable with the largest dilator, continue the regimen at least once a week if you aren't having sex regularly.

And don't forget the moisturizers.

It takes patience and diligence to rehab your bottom, but you can do it. With a little TLC, everything will work as well as it ever did and sex can be every bit as luscious as it ever was.

QUESTIONS... AND ANSWERS

Q: Why do I have pain and hypersensitivity?

What you describe—pain and a burning sensation around your clitoris—is most consistent with vulvovaginal atrophy. As we lose estrogen, the genital tissues thin, and the labia and clitoris actually become smaller. There's also less blood supply to the genitals. Beyond making arousal and orgasm more difficult to achieve, these changes can also lead to discomfort, and experiencing pain when you're looking for pleasure will certainly affect your sex drive and arousal!

Localized estrogen is the option that works best (and it's often a huge difference) for most of my patients, restoring tissues and comfort. Talk to your health care provider about the available options and what you might consider in choosing one.

A vaginal moisturizer can also help you restore those tissues, but I suspect you'll find that most effective in combination with localized estrogen.

Please do take steps to address your symptoms! If sex can be more comfortable and enjoyable for you, I'm hopeful that your sex drive will rebound.

Q: Any suggestions for overcoming lack of desire and pain during sex?

The first thing I try to do with women who have both of these issues is to make sex comfortable. It is pretty hard to be interested in intercourse when you know it is going to lead to pain.

You might consider vaginal estrogen–estrogen that is 'localized' rather than 'systemic' and is delivered only to the vagina. This would require a prescription product. Or you need to commit to using a vaginal moisturizer consistently; this reintroduces moisture to the vagina on an ongoing basis.

Once sex is comfortable, then approach the issue of desire, which admittedly, is difficult. Yours might be a situation in which to consider using testosterone or buproprion, an antidepressant that can have the side effect of increasing desire. Engaging mindfulness and choosing sex is important to the sexual relationship. I review Basson's research with patients, and remind them that desire does not play as big a role in women's sexuality at this stage of life, so being intentional and choosing to engage is often necessary.

Find a provider you trust to talk through some of these issues and begin to explore options.

Q: What's the difference between lubricants and moisturizers?

The real difference between a lubricant and a moisturizer is duration. Lubricants coat the vagina to ease penetration, which adds comfort during intercourse. They provide a benefit at the time of use, but are not designed to last.

Moisturizers are designed to be longer lasting. They replenish and help maintain water content in the vagina, clinging to the vaginal walls so they are effective for several days. Mineral- and vegetable-oil-based moisturizers are not recommended because they can cause irritation, providing a habitat for abnormal bacteria. Vitamin E oil, on the other hand, can be a helpful ingredient.

Yes, one moisturizer option we've found popular at MiddlesexMD, can be applied as a vaginal moisturizer every 3 days. Some women prefer more frequent use, others need it a little less often to stay comfortable. You can determine your own frequency with use.

Q: How can I apply moisturizer more conveniently?

Like a number of my patients, you'd like to avoid the disposable applicator that often comes with vaginal moisturizers—whether for environmental or cost reasons (or both!). I know many women prefer to use an applicator: no muss, no fuss. I can't help but encourage women to reconsider the simplest approach: Wash your hands, apply moisturizer to your finger, and insert it in your vagina. This has a number of advantages—you're experienced in washing your hands, your finger is warm and able to curve with your vagina, and you'll know your body better. If you've used tampons without applicators or menstrual sponges or cups, you may be entirely comfortable with this method.

But I know our instinctive preferences are hard to retrain. Another alternative that's worked for patients is to go to the drugstore and check out the syringes for one of appropriate size and cleanability. Note that these are typically designed for single use, so you'll need to develop your own approach for washing and storing the syringe between uses.

Find a method that works for you! Vaginal moisturizer makes a difference with regular use.

Q: Can I get an over-the-counter estrogen cream for vaginal dryness?

Estrogen-containing vaginal preparations are prescription only. If you haven't tried lubricants and moisturizers, which are available over the counter, you might try those first.

Lubricants are designed for short-term effect, to make intercourse immediately more comfortable. They can be water-based, silicon-based, or a hybrid of the two.

Vaginal moisturizers are designed for longer-term maintenance of your vaginal tissues. They don't contain hormones, so don't require a prescription. They're typically used every several days.

Localized estrogen, which is available as a ring or vaginal tablet in addition to cream, helps to increase blood flow and elasticity in genital tissues. If you've tried lubricants and moisturizers and haven't yet been comfortable during sex, consider talking to your health care provider to see if localized estrogen or another hormone therapy might be right for you.

Q: Why am I 'hitting a wall' with sex?

What you describe–feeling like your partner is "hitting a wall" when you attempt intercourse, sounds most consistent with vaginismus. A physical exam can look normal; with careful palpation of the pelvic floor muscles, you can feel them tightening, which is what makes the "wall."

You might go back to your physician with the specific question, "Do my pelvic floor muscles seem too tight?" If that is the case, dilators and/or physical therapy are good solutions. A dilator set will include much smaller sizes–as small as a half-inch–so you can increase your comfort gradually.

Good luck! This is an issue you and your partner can work through.

CHAPTER FIVE

THAT LOVING FEELING

As we grow older, we have less blood flow and less sensitivity in our genital tissues. We're not as quick to become aroused. A woman may interpret the lack of arousal as a sign that she just should give up on sex. But we hope she doesn't take it that way!

We don't give up reading when our eyesight gets worse — we get a pair of reading glasses. We can compensate by taking more time, energy, and attention to awaken or re-awaken our sensations. Using tools — vibrators, warming lubricants, or clitoral pumps — is an excellent way to increase self-awareness and sensation.

FEMALE ANATOMY 101

This post was contributed by Julie, a member of the MiddlesexMD team.

Writing for my gynecologist friend has included a lot of Aha! moments. I admit some of this learning makes me blush. It's not just because I blush when talking about sex—though I do. It's because I'm embarrassed when I'm caught not knowing things I think I should have known a long, long time ago.

So, I'm reading along in Dr. Barb's enormous textbooks on female sexuality, when I come across an illustration of the clitoris, sort of like the one below. I nearly passed it over, because, what's to know at my age? I've lived with this equipment for 50 years. I'd like to think I know my way around it.

But this illustration colored in the entire structure of the clitoris. Not just the glans, but also the shaft and the crus clitoris, or crura.

Excuse me… the shaft?… and the crura?

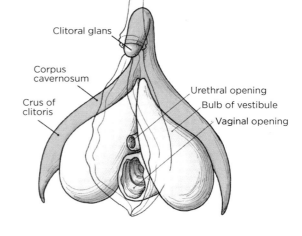

No.. please picture me picking my head up like a prairie dog, looking around my office, and asking the air…

"The shaft?!"

"And the crura!?!"

Somehow in all my curious, bookish, research-happy past, I never learned more about the clitoris than about the little button—the glans—the part that sticks out from the prepuce at the top of the labia.

Who knew my clitoris had legs? And a shaft, even?

But yes, indeed. It's practically a little penis under that hood. With long, long legs that extend waaay back toward the perineum, which fill with blood when I'm aroused.

Now, of course, the cool, rational part of my mind tells me I have enjoyed my crura—and possibly even the shaft—because they've been there all along. But I would have liked to know about them from the start. I can't help but wish for a few years back in which I could quite clearly visualize my long, leggy crura.

What can we do with this information? Well, with age, the clitoris loses some sensitivity. We may find it useful to use warming oils and gels or vibrating sex aids to increase stimulation to the clitoris as we prepare for or engage in sex.

And of course, to do that, it really does help to know where it is.

Back to the books...

THE BIG O (AND WE DON'T MEAN OPRAH!)

Orgasm. Such a complicated topic; so many questions, so few answers. But let's focus on the most important point, which is, that for women, the biggest obstacle to experiencing orgasm is anxiety. How can anyone relax while having sex if she's thinking, "Will it happen this time or won't it?"

As you can imagine, research on this topic is somewhat limited. But the renowned sex researchers William Masters and Virginia Johnson, who were the first to describe the four-step process of experiencing orgasm (during intercourse) many decades ago, said there are four steps involved:

1. Excitement. During foreplay, blood begins to engorge the clitoris, vagina, and nipples, and creates a full body sexual blush. Heart rate and blood pressure increase.

2. Plateau. Sexual tension builds as a precursor to orgasm. The outer one-third of the vagina becomes particularly engorged with blood, creating what's called "the orgasmic platform." Heart rate, blood pressure, and respiration continue to increase.

3. Orgasm. A series of rhythmic contractions occur in the uterus, vagina, and the pelvic floor muscles. Sexual tension releases, and muscles throughout the body may contract. A feeling of warmth usually emanates from the pelvis and spreads throughout the entire body.

4. Resolution. The body relaxes, with blood flowing away from the engorged sexual organs. Heart rate, blood pressure, and respiration return to normal.

(For another model of sexual arousal, remember Rosemary Basson's, which takes into account women's more complicated reality [see p. 5].)

Another good thing to know is that experiencing orgasm during intercourse takes time. In one study of 1,000 women, the "mean duration" was about 13 minutes. So trying to hurry it along or time it to coincide with your partner's is probably not going to help.

It all gets back to the whole idea of relaxing—of letting go and focusing on the moment, enjoying the closeness and intimacy itself without worrying about what the outcome will be every time you have sex.

And, too, most women—two thirds of us—never experience orgasm at all during intercourse; some say the only way they ever get there it is through hand stimulation (their own or their partner's) or with a vibrator, which often is the quickest route.

If you're having trouble experiencing orgasm, try some things on your own to see what works and what doesn't, not just physically, but mentally. Some women, for example, find that fantasizing puts them in a "zone" where they can escape the distractions of life. (Imagine yourself on a desert island with the one you love!)

This is one of those things that can only get better with honest, open communication. Talk with your partner about your feelings, your reactions—everything—so that you both have a good understanding of what's going on and why. And in the meantime, relax and enjoy the journey.

HER FIRST VIBRATOR

"A Vibrator? Me? At my age?!"

That's a pretty common response when I recommend—actually prescribe—using a vibrator to the patients I see in my menopause

Chapter Five: That Loving Feeling

practice. In my small city in the middle of the Midwest sex aids are of course in use—as they are everywhere and for millennia—but they are hard to find and almost never openly discussed, at least not among the generation hitting menopause right now.

But, yes, Virginia, a vibrator, for you, and especially now. Here's why: As we approach menopause, our sex hormones are in a constant state of flux. Perhaps flooding our systems one minute, depleted the next. What they are, especially, is unreliable. They are just not reliably there when you need them to do their work in bringing you to arousal, helping to lubricate your vagina, to make sex possible, much less pleasurable.

Then, once we have fully reached menopause, our hormones are more predictable, but they're in shorter supply. That might not bring any measurable sexual changes for one woman, but for another, it can feel like a door has been shut in her face. Her vaginal tissues may not respond to the same sexual stimulation that always worked in the past. That can leave some of us feeling as if we have just stopped functioning, sexually.

Of course, the whole point of this book and MiddlesexMD and my medical practice is to share the news that it ain't over until you say it's over. The secret to keeping sex alive after menopause is *more*. Follow our recipe: More knowledge, more lubrication, more stimulation, more intimacy, more exercise.

What came without trying when we were young—reading the small print, responding to sexual stimuli—now requires assistive devices. Reading glasses... and a vibrator. (And moisturizers, maybe dilators, a sexy movie or two, a pillow?...)

But especially vibrators. And not just any vibrator, but a vibrator with more power and endurance than a young girl needs. Clitoral stimulation at our age needs to overcome the sluggish circulation in a clitoris that, if unused, will go dormant, pulling up into the body. Our vibrators need more power, over a longer period, to replace that circulation and encourage a clitoris to come out to play.

Of course, I can explain why we need more vulvo-vaginal stimulation at our age to nearly any woman in my office, and she may understand and fully accept what I'm telling her. But her next step is to go home and discuss this with her partner, if she has one.

Many times, at our age, we're talking about spouses—sexual partners we've had for a very long time. And if that sexual partnership has not included the use of any sexual aids, bringing that first vibrator to bed can be a daunting change.

The truth is, we don't know how our partners will respond to our need or desire to use a vibrator until we raise the subject. One good way to do that is to say—"Well, Dr. Barb said this could help." Show your partner this book, read it together; browse MiddlesexMD.com together, where you'll find lots of information that can help you communicate what your body is going through and what you and your partner can do about it to continue to enjoy your sex life.

It can help to shop for your first vibrator together, whether in a store or online. What I look for to offer women in my practice and through MiddlesexMD are especially well-suited to women in midlife, who need vibrators that will hold a long charge and deliver a strong vibration.

But even with all this information at the ready, one or both of you may be suffering from some vibrator mythology that will make you hesitate to use one of these devices. So let me do a little dispelling:

MYTH 1: VIBRATORS ARE FOR PEOPLE WHOSE RELATIONSHIPS AREN'T STRONG. Actually, vibrators work best for couples whose intimacy is solid and secure, playful and creative. Introducing a vibrator at our age can awaken those qualities in a strong relationship, and underscore an important lesson, that the nature of our sexuality shifts as we age, period. Accepting that with grace and creativity is important for any partnership. To do otherwise strikes me as being like refusing to use a pacemaker or an artificial valve.

MYTH 2: VIBRATORS MAKE IT HARD TO HAVE AN ORGASM ANY OTHER WAY. The exact opposite is true. The more orgasms women have, the more easily we can achieve them. Every orgasm helps to strengthen the muscles and nerve pathways that ready us for our next one. While, having easier orgasms with a vibrator may encourage its regular use, no vibrator can ever replace human contact. Women generally crave intimacy first.

MYTH 3: VIBRATORS ARE FOR MASTURBATION. Okay, this one is true—but it's not true that they're only for masturbation. They have gone mainstream among couples who have figured out that vibrators are great for stimulating every erogenous zone, and in addition to the boost they give women, are particularly good for stimulating a man's prostate. They are great for foreplay, during sex, and for gentle stimulation after intercourse, too.

MYTH 4: VIBRATORS ARE FOR SEX MANIACS. Sex maniacs may like them. But so may your neighbor, your pastor, your doctor, your auto mechanic. We've been using electronic vibrators since we harnessed electricity, In fact, steam-powered vibrating devices (yikes!) were patented in the 1860s and 1870s; the first electromechanical device was designed in 1880. The earliest vibrator was intended for massage of men's skeletal muscles, but doctors soon found they were useful for a broad range of "female ailments": female hysteria, pelvic pain, nervous tension, and a number of gynecological complaints. It's true that vibrators gained something of an "illicit" reputation around the 1920s, but more recently they've become much more mainstream than you might expect—including being recommended by doctors (like me!) as "adjunctive medical accessories" to restore or enhance sexual response.

Shopping for vibrators can be fun, and really very interesting. These devices come in many configurations and with many options, because, well, we're all different. What one woman or couple likes and needs can be a real turnoff for the next.

When my team and I shopped for the collection we offer at our online store, we kept these factors in mind:

SIZE AND SHAPE
Vibrators come in sizes and shapes destined for specific as well as general use. You will find mini vibrators great for clitoral and prostate stimulation; they'll likely fit in the palm of your hand.

There are larger clitoral vibrators shaped to cup the clitoris and labia. These can be combined with a dilator or dildo, used during intercourse, or used on their own to help stimulate vulvo-vaginal tissues.

Midsized vibrators are often wand-shaped for vaginal and g-spot stimulation. Large women find these useful for the reach they provide, and they can also provide leverage for women who have difficulty with hand strength.

Massagers are dual use devices, used for vulvar stimulation as well as massaging muscles anywhere in the body (really!). Attachments for these devices can transform them into vaginal and g-spot stimulating wonders.

POWER
Older women generally need more power, both a stronger vibration and a longer session time. For that reason, rechargeable devices are usually a better bet than those that use disposable batteries, although there are some in that category that have plenty of power.

MATERIALS
Hard plastics and stainless steel are easy to clean. Look for materials that are guaranteed to be phthalate-free. Silicone surfaces are wonderfully warm to the touch, with a skin-like feel. They clean up with soap and water or with cleaners made especially for sex aids, but owners need to be careful not to use them with silicone-based lubricants. Some manufacturers now use antimicrobial plastics, medical-grade materials formulated to discourage bacterial growth.

If that's too many variables to maneuver in one shopping experience, may we make a recommendation? If this is your first vibrator ever, why not start with one designed specifically for clitoral and labial stimulation? That way you're sure to have a device that will help you improve circulation, keeping your vulvar tissues responsive and ready for sex when you are.

When you have your new device in hand, charge it fully before you use it. Start slowly and gently, using plenty of lubricant, learning what your device will do and how your body likes it. If it's been awhile since you have had any sexual stimulation at all, be patient. Give your body time and a number of sessions to awaken to this new sensation. And if you're bringing this new toy into an old relationship, talk through it, explore this device together. The more communication, the better.

DR. KRYCHMAN'S "MEET YOUR VIBRATOR"

In the course of a conversation about vibrators, I asked MiddlesexMD medical advisor Dr. Michael Krychman how he recommends that his patients begin to use a vibrator. Here's what he says:

Get to know your vibrator. Take it out of the package and learn how it works, how to charge it or what kind of batteries it takes. When it's charged, play with the buttons, turn it on and off. How many speeds and settings does it have? Wash your vibrator well before using it; use warm water with a mild soap and rinse it well so that no residual soap remains. If it isn't waterproof, be careful not to get any water near the battery case. Check for sharp edges or seams.

Start on your own. Even if you're planning to use your vibrator with a partner, it's a good idea to check it out by yourself first. You'll feel less self-conscious and you can really concentrate on how it feels. Make sure you have enough time and privacy. If you have roommates, children, thin walls, or nosy neighbors, turn on some music, shut the blinds, and use blankets and comforters to mute the sound.

Play with the lights turned on. Not everyone is comfortable with this suggestion, but I think playing with a vibrator with the lights on can be very educational and useful. You can discover specific places on your body that are rich with nerve endings and ready for enjoyment and stimulation. You can use this information yourself and share with a lover when you're ready.

Turn the vibrator off before you turn it on. Get comfortable with the feel of the vibrator on your body. Run it along your body without even turning it on. Notice how it feels. Press it firmly against your skin; press it onto your body and massage your muscles. If the vibrator is made of a hard material this will probably feel nice. If the vibrator is a soft rubber and doesn't feel smooth against your skin, try it on top of your clothing. This isn't meant to give you an orgasm, but it's a gentle and non-threatening way to introduce your body to the vibrator.

Move your vibrator from the outside in. Once you turn it on, start by touching the vibrator to your body; this will help you understand the vibration sensation. Even though vibrators are used mostly around the vulva and clitoris, get a feel for the vibration all over your body, including touching the breasts and other areas that feel good. Slowly move to the more sensitive parts of your body.

Don't be in a rush: Explore every part of your body. Vibrators never get tired, and they let you explore every inch of your body for sexual pleasure. Many women find that one side or one part of their clitoris responds to vibration more than another. Don't rush: Leaving a vibrator in place can allow it to establish sensation connections that previously weren't there. Adjust the speed, pressure, and angle of the vibrator. Most vibrators have multiple speed settings; always start on low and work your way up. Experiment with applying different pressure. You may enjoy a lot of deep pressure with clitoral stimulation.

Most women use vibrators for external stimulation, but as long as your vibrator is safe for it, there's no reason not to try penetration. While far more nerve endings are outside the vagina than inside, lots of women enjoy penetration with a vibrator. A vibrator that is safe for penetration will be smooth, have no rough edges, and won't absorb bodily fluids. Again, start slow and get yourself aroused by using the vibrator externally first.

There are just two things I caution women about: First, make sure you're using the right lubricant with a vibrator. Silicone-based lubricants will degrade silicone vibrators. And if you're sharing your vibrator outside of a monogamous relationship, put a condom on it.

Sounds like good advice! And getting acquainted with a vibrator yourself will help you introduce it to your partner, too–which I'll focus on next.

Chapter Five: That Loving Feeling

VIBRATORS FOR TWO

My conversations with patients, blog readers, and visitors to MiddlesexMD tell me that once a person's gotten past her own discomfort with the idea of a vibrator, there can lurk another obstacle: How to introduce it to intimacy with a partner.

I've heard from both men and women on this topic: Both have asked how to introduce a vibrator into a relationship or how to overcome resistance. A recent study done at the Center for Sexual Health Promotion at Indiana University suggests some couples have figured it out. Half of both men and women have used a vibrator with a partner at least once. Slightly more men than women agree that vibrators can make sex with a partner more exciting, but for both the number is close to 60 percent.

And we know from other research that about two-thirds of women don't experience orgasm with penetration alone; the IU study says half of women agree that a vibrator helps.

But in spite of that evidence that couples are using vibrators, and that women find them satisfying, there's still resistance. I talked to Mary Jo Rapini, psychotherapist and a MiddlesexMD advisors, to learn more.

The first issue for some women is their preconceptions, Mary Jo says. "If you think of vibrators—or any other part of sex—as 'creepy,' you're showing resistance. Resistance is a product of your own thoughts, which means you can change it and open yourself up to communication and growth. My first request would be that she use the word 'uncomfortable.' This opens up a wonderful conversation—if you're uncomfortable with something, you can add something else to lovemaking, and not necessarily all at once. You might not be comfortable with a vibrator, but you may like being massaged during lovemaking with wonderful massage oil. Lovemaking is exciting and it's so healthy for the heart, immune system, and hormone levels; I encourage women—and couples—to try new things, slowly, without rejecting the concept of lovemaking with new items."

"Women are sometimes reluctant to own their own sexuality," Mary Jo says, which works against introducing a vibrator—and other things—into a couple's intimacy.

"Men are so visual in regards to sex," Mary Jo says. "Many men enjoy watching their partner masturbate with a vibrator—especially if their partner is able to enjoy it. Men love watching the woman they love enjoy sex. They also want to please the woman. When the woman is able to let the man hold the vibrator for her, or use it gently on him, he begins to see the benefits.

"He may feel rejected if she prefers the vibrator to him, but including him and showing him what feels best being touched is a big turn-on for men. If she can talk about what feels good, how she likes to be touched, the intimacy will be a thousand times stronger."

The IU study, by the way, confirms that seventy percent of men don't find a vibrator intimidating during sex.

But that may be beside the point. The real focus, Mary Jo says, is something different: "Sex is not about the penis or vagina, but your ability to let go, explore, and broaden your awareness and understanding of your sexual self—and your partner. Being able to express yourself sexually and feeling safe and secure in that relationship heightens your health both physically and emotionally."

THE G-SPOT: DEFINED BUT NOT DEMYSTIFIED

Remember the G-spot brouhaha?

Yes, there is one. No, there isn't. Is. Isn't.

If you were aware of that controversy you might wonder whatever happened to it. Was anything about the mysterious G-spot ever resolved?

For all intents and purposes, after a flurry of attention in the 1980s, the G-spot seemed to go underground for a decade or two, but lately, with the advent of newfangled imaging devices, the search for the G-spot

Chapter Five: That Loving Feeling

has resurrected once again. So, in case you've been wondering, let us bring you up to date on this mysterious region.

The G-spot is defined (and yes, there is a definition) as an erogenous area about the size of a nickel located 2 to 3 inches inside the front wall of a woman's vagina.

The name comes from the German gynecologist Ernst Gräfenberg, who first wrote about its existence in 1950. But a mysterious pleasure center in roughly the same place had also been mentioned in ancient Indian texts and by Regnier de Graaf, a Dutch physician, in 1672, who wrote that secretions from this area "lubricate their sexual parts in agreeable fashion during coitus."

But it was the publication of *The G-Spot and Other Discoveries about Human Sexuality* in the 1980s that ignited a frenzy. Couples contorted themselves into pretzels seeking the elusive mind-blowing orgasms that accompanied just the right stimulation. (Leaving many women feeling inadequate and their partners frustrated, I'm sure.) Researchers, too, overheated their Bunsen burners trying to find the darned thing.

Then, without further fuel to fan the fire, the short attention span of popular culture wandered, and interest in the G-spot waned.

In 2008, however, Italian researchers using new ultrasound technology discovered a thickened area on the front vaginal wall of about half of 20 women. Women with this thickened tissue were more likely to experience vaginal orgasms. In 2010, a group of British researchers asked 90 pairs of twins if they had a "so called G-spot, a small area the size of a 20p coin on the front wall of your vagina that is sensitive to deep pressure?"

Unsurprisingly, given the subjective nature of that question, the results from the British study were ambiguous and were challenged by other scientists. The following month French researchers, askance at the sloppy work from the boys across the channel, declared that 56 percent of women did indeed have "un point G."

Physiologically, a G-spot has not been definitively identified by gynecologists, nor in dissections nor consistently in ultrasounds. So the mystery remains, according to urologist Dr. Amichai Kilchevsky, who led an extensive review of all research on the issue. "Without a doubt, a discrete anatomic entity called the G-spot does not exist," says Dr. Kilchevsky.

Yet, women consistently report that stimulating the front of the vaginal wall produces a deep, pleasurable orgasm. "…it has been pretty widely accepted that many women find it pleasurable, if not orgasmic, to be stimulated on the front wall of the vagina," said Debby Herbenick, researcher at Indiana University and author of Because It Feels Good.

According to Australian researcher Dr. Helen O'Connell, the clitoris, urethra, and vagina all work together during sexual stimulation, creating a "clitoral complex." Since the urethra lies along the outside of the vagina and the clitoris has deep "roots" within the vaginal walls it's no stretch to imagine that all the parts work together during sex.

Some doctors compare the G-spot controversy to obsession over penis size—much ado about nothing. Lots of women don't orgasm with vaginal penetration alone; indeed, most of us need both vaginal and clitoral stimulation to orgasm. So, if "we don't even have orgasm all figured out yet, I don't know why we would expect to have the G-spot figured out," Herbenick said in an article on Netdoctor.

Because of its approximate location, the G-spot is devilishly hard to reach, especially in the standard missionary position. However, if you'd like to spice up your bedtime routine with a little research of your own, try sitting astride your partner, on a sturdy chair or firm surface. Lean backward so the penis has a better chance of connecting with the front of the vagina.

If this sounds too acrobatic for a fun Friday night, you can always fall back on the trusty index finger. Lie on your back while your partner inserts his finger, using a "come hither" motion to stimulate the front of the vagina. Or try a toy. Special G-spot vibrators are available that are longer with a kink at the end. Results are still mixed, so focus on the exploration, not a specific result.

And remember to be well-lubricated and relaxed. Light a few candles and some incense. Research has never been so fun. Just keep in mind that while theories of the G-spot are great, so is experimenting with your own sensations, in a spirit of creativity. Don't assume there's a "should" or an "ought" that you're missing. Embrace your own personal sexuality!

WHEN AN ORGASM IS NOT AN ORGASM

This topic comes up more often with girlfriends than with patients. But it comes up often enough with girlfriends that I know it's on my patients' minds, too! The question is whether it's sometimes okay to fake an orgasm.

I think it depends on how you define "sometimes"—and what your reasons are for faking. Let's start by acknowledging that, by some estimates, as many as one in ten of us has never achieved an orgasm. Among those of us who orgasm, we might do so in only about half of our sexual encounters. And, just to dispel one widespread myth, only about a third of us achieve orgasms with heterosexual intercourse alone.

All that said, I think you get to decide when you signal your partner that you've achieved orgasm when you haven't. Maybe you're getting tired but you don't want to break the intimate mood. Maybe you want to satisfy or boost your partner's confidence. Studies show that nearly 80 percent of women will fake orgasm at some point.

But making a habit of it isn't fair to you or to your partner, even though, with our busy, fast-paced lives, it can be an easy pattern to fall into. It's worth it to spend some time—alone and with your partner—learning more about your body and its paths to orgasm. Even if you've had a lot of experience, changes in hormone levels, circulation, and tissue health can mean your needs have changed.

If you're faking more than once in a great while, there may be something else going on that needs attention. Do you feel like it takes too long to reach orgasm? Does your partner know exactly what to do to help you achieve an orgasm? Is there something on your mind that's making it hard to relax when you're having sex? There are lots of ways to increase your mindfulness, sensation, and response.

We like sex for lots of reasons, and orgasm doesn't have to be one of them. If you've never learned to have an orgasm, or if you don't have them regularly, don't consider yourself a sexual failure! But if you're finding yourself pretending more than you used to, it's never too late to learn or relearn our bodies.

WARMING OILS AND LUBRICANTS: HOT TOPICALS

As we age, along with everything else we lose (our keys, our glasses, our hearing), it's common to lose sensation in our genitals. Less sensation makes it harder to achieve arousal, which can lead to becoming less interested in sex. Blame it on lower hormone levels. One easy, inexpensive, and often fun way to stimulate the genital area is with warming oils or lubricants.

There's a reason why when we become aroused, we feel "hot." Blood flows to the genital area, creating a flush of warmth. Warming oils or lubricants are products that cause a chemical reaction when applied to the skin. They create a sensation of warmth that simulates the heat of arousal. It's intended to feel good and to give us a little "leg up" to actual arousal.

Warming oils and lubricants may contain minty or peppery ingredients, or they may contain natural herbs, spices, or even vitamins that cause a warming chemical reaction. Some may have added flavors or colors.

Use these warming products on healthy, intact tissue; don't use them if you have any irritation or abrasion in your genital area. It's also important to test a small area to make sure you like the feeling and don't have an allergic reaction.

Warming lubricants that are water-based can be applied as you would any lubricant—a generous tablespoonful to your own or your partner's genitals.

Warming oils are intended to be used only externally. Inside, they're not conducive to good vaginal health, and they can also degrade the latex in a condom. You can spread warming oils on the labia, over the clitoral hood, and around the vaginal area. Some women like to include their nipples. Men like it, too, but avoid using oils on the penis if there's a chance of vaginal penetration.

In addition to their practical function, warming lubricants or oils can add an element of shared pleasure to your sex life. And that can be arousing, too.

WHAT DO BREASTS DO FOR US?

Recently I treated a patient who'd had elective breast reduction surgery. Nerve damage during the procedure had caused her to lose all sensation in her nipples. She found herself unable to have an orgasm without the extra stimulation those nerves had provided. That was a consequence she hadn't thought to ask about!

Changes in nipple sensation are possible side effects of any type of breast surgery, including elective surgery to increase or reduce breast size. Sometimes the effects are temporary, but they can be permanent. It's important to understand these risks—and the role your breasts play in sexual arousal and satisfaction—when choosing breast surgery for cosmetic reasons. I don't know if my patient would have made a different choice, but she may have.

How do breasts contribute to orgasm? Some women (not most) can reach orgasm through nipple stimulation alone. Others rely on intense breast and nipple fondling to "put them over the top" during oral sex or vaginal penetration.

Like the clitoris, nipples are bundles of nerve endings that respond to touch by releasing certain hormones in the brain. One of these hormones, oxytocin, is sometimes referred to as the "cuddle hormone": It makes us feel warm and open toward the person whose touch initiated its release in our bodies. Other hormones, including testosterone and endorphins, combine to create a surge of sexual arousal that increases blood flow to the clitoris and stimulates vaginal lubrication.

For most women, sexual foreplay is essential to getting us interested in and ready for intercourse or penetration. And for most women (82 percent in one study) breast and nipple stimulation are an essential ingredient of foreplay. We talk a lot about clitoral stimulation and vaginal maintenance for maintaining our sexual satisfaction, but other parts of our bodies also play a part in arousal and orgasm, though.

For those of us fortunate enough to retain the pleasant sensations our breasts can provide, remembering these important sites of arousal during foreplay and intercourse (warming and massage oils can work wonders here) will enhance our readiness for and enjoyment of sex—at any age.

SEEING RED

This post contributed by MiddlesexMD team member Julie.

Squeezies. The year was 1986, maybe. Or 1987. I'm not exactly sure, and precision is not important to this story. It matters only that it was the last day of the year. My sister and I were young, married, without our husbands, working hard, very tired, and feeling a little bit entitled to a good time, or as good as we could have without regrets.

I was visiting her in the college town where her husband was pursuing his graduate degree and where she was working a horrible job to keep them in their crappy apartment. He was off visiting family. And the apartment just wasn't festive enough for a new year's celebration.

We were confused about what to do. We didn't want to foist ourselves onto other couples our age, bent on a romantic evening. We didn't belong in a gang of single people, either. But we were so young, and wanted to feel pretty and desirable and giddy and all those things women of any age like to feel.

Precisely speaking, we wanted men to read our wedding bands and weep.

Chapter Five: That Loving Feeling

We had a standing joke all through those years when we were becoming less and less sure of our appeal. One of us would call, and the other would respond:

Caller: "Well it's not as if I couldn't get laid by another man if I wanted to."

Resp: "Of course you could."

Caller: "I mean, I've still got it."

Resp: "Always did. Always will."

Caller: "For instance, I could walk into that truck stop there, right now, and I bet someone would do me."

Resp: "Absolutely. And it wouldn't cost you that much either."

Caller: "Not too much."

And then we would laugh and wonder, really, would it cost so very much? But we were very good girls. Fidelity always mattered to us. But we wondered...

I mentioned my sister's terrible job. I think it's a job no longer held by anyone, actually. She was laying out ads in that city's big daily newspaper. It was a transient's job and one of her transient co-workers had shared her method for getting all the sexual attention a girl could ever want.

It seems beauty had nothing to do with it. What a woman needed to do was exude sexual power. And the way to do that, she said, is this: You walk into a room. You pause. You squeeze your vaginal muscles, very hard. And you think, "Red."

That's it.

That is, you envision that color. A vivid red. The color of blood, of passion. Bring it into your mind. Fill your awareness with Red. All while squeezing. Hard.

So.

That New Year's evening, armed with this information, our plan was clear. We would head downtown, find a hopping bar or club. Upscale. Nice. Walk in. Squeeze. Red.

Did I mention that we were in Virginia? Yes, well, that detail does matter. So when I say that a soft little puffy bit of snow had begun to fall as we left her little apartment, you have the right sort of unease taking root in your gut.

Virginia just does not do snow. We sisters are from northern Michigan, where an inch of snow means nothing. Two inches may bring a comment. But we need four to six inches at a single drop before we begin to wonder about the state of the roads. Virginia falls apart at the first flake. A half an inch will have Virginians filling their bathtubs with water, seeking out candles and flashlights.

And apparently that's just what all the Virginians in this town were doing as we hit downtown, looking for a party, our hot-roller-set hair lacquered up, wearing our Calvin Klein jeans and high heels.

We were aware that there was very little traffic. Well, none. Anywhere. We noted that many restaurants, bars, and clubs were closed. But our heads were just too full of our plans and our youth to connect the dots, it seems.

We stopped for cigarettes, I remember, at a 7-11, where the counter lady said she hoped we would get home safely. That didn't really register with us, though. On we went until we finally found an open bar. Cash and cigarettes in our cute little purses, we parked and slogged through slush into the bar.

Right.

Three steps in, we stopped for a half beat...

That moment wasn't quite long enough to register that there were only three people in the place, two of them customers who were clearly the profit base for the bar—old, colorless men in colorless clothes sitting

Chapter Five: That Loving Feeling

very still, drinking intently, not looking around, but straight ahead into their pasts.

We squeezed hard enough to wobble on our heels. We filled the bar with a steamy red awareness. And then...

Well, I seem to remember that I started things by snorting, and then choking, and maybe a little spittle landed on my sister's chin. My sister's runny nose released in that moment, and we both fell against one another and into empty chairs, unable to breathe for several long minutes while we laughed until tears rolled and mucus spewed and spit flew from our various orifices.

The men, indeed, all turned to stare. The bartender, looking as if he wouldn't serve us anyway, said the bar would be closing early because of the storm.

"Uh, what storm?" we wondered. And that sealed the deal. We would have to go.

Deflated, dragging our fingers through our wet, sticky curls, we slipped and slid back to our cars, realizing, finally, that this town had no plows. No salt. No infrastructure for snow. And home was all uphill.

Squeezies. Almost 30 years later, squeezies (Kegel exercises now) are no longer just an option for women our age. We do them to keep continent, to maintain the muscles that let us enjoy orgasms, to keep organs in their rightful places. No longer a scheme for attention-getting, we do them in check-out lines, at traffic lights, waiting for trains, for kids, for grandchildren.

But I can never do my squeezies without a smile. Or Seeing Red. Or remembering hot rollers and high heels and laughing until the snot ran free.

NEED HELP WITH KEGELS?

This post contributed by MiddlesexMD team member Julie.

Of course you do your kegels, daily as suggested. You're probably doing them right now.

No? No. Me either. Nor yesterday. Not while stopped in traffic. Not while commuting. Not while waiting in the grocery line, or any of the zillion times or places I've been advised to do them.

And when I do get around to them, I have kegel ADD or something. I'm too easily distracted to do them well enough, thoroughly enough, or regularly enough.

And yet, there isn't a better, cheaper, more useful tool in our arsenal for keeping our sex muscles fit and our bladders under control.

My last big sneezing fit while at dinner with friends had me renewing my determination to do better, though.

If you're in my boat, you may want to start with a kegel exercise tool. A set of benwa balls or a kegel weight. Especially for beginners, a little weight in the vagina makes it really easy to isolate the correct muscles, and understand which muscles we need to work. Kegel weights can help maintain patency of the vagina, and they help strengthen orgasms, if you slowly increase the weight of the kegel device over time.

(Note: You won't want to use the barbell while waiting in traffic or in line at the grocery store. Is that clear, friends? Use these at home, on your own time, please…;-)

Weights in hand, what I need is time and focus and coaching. And ladies, there is an App for that. That is, if you use an iPhone or iTouch, you can download Kegel coaching applications for anywhere from free to about $5. I've found three currently available. They're very different, and all helpful—and while there may be different options available for you, since app options change all the time, these descriptions might help you decide what you're looking for.

Chapter Five: That Loving Feeling

KEGELTOPIA, $4.99. With a Kegel primer on board to help you learn about and understand the exercises, Kegeltopia has several exercise types to choose from—mini kegels, 3-second holds, elevator, and freestyle—and the ability to track your total Kegel time over days, weeks, and months. Designed particularly for pre- and post-pregnancy, this is the current Cadillac of Kegel apps. The voice coach is a woman, with a lovely, calm demeanor. She uses chimes to help cue you along, calling to your inner yogi. Nothing to distract you here. It's all pink and flowery and girly.

KEGEL EXERCISE APP, $.99. This is a clever app so generic looking no one looking over your shoulder on the subway or in the grocery line would guess what you were up to. A straightforward timer developed to help prompt you to hold and release your PC muscles for several reps, which is a general guideline repeated by most Kegel instructors. I love the simplicity of this app. Love the merciful pause button. The simple two-tone cues for squeezing and resting. I can reset both the squeeze and release time to start out more slowly if the default time is too much, or increase slowly as I get stronger. Also this app feels more appropriate for both men and women. A nice app for doing your Kegels together. (Yes, it's a good idea for men to do Kegels to maintain good prostate and urinary health, also to help learn to control ejaculation.) My inner geek likes this app best for the simple functionality and the price.

PC-FITNESS APP, Free. I think it's awfully nice that this app writer went to the trouble, and it is free, after all. It's got three exercise modes, 2-second squeezes with 1-second rests between, 15-second squeezes with 5-second rests between (useful for elevator up exercises, I think), and olympic-level 60-second squeezes with 60-second rests between. You can set your preferred number of reps. There is no pause button. The controls aren't as intuitive as the one for the simple Kegel Exercise App, but read the instructions, and you'll find its function out pretty quickly.

Right. Nothing to stop me now...

For more on how and why to do your kegels, find more information on our website.

PATIENCE, PATIENCE!

So you arrive home from a hectic day at the office, and there's the box you've been waiting for, with your new lube, a vaginal moisturizer, and those dilators that have promised to return your sex life from painful to normal. "Oh boy!" you think. "Orgasm tonight!"

Please, please, please, slow down. I know it's hard to wait when you've been anxious to find an answer.

The conditions that cause painful intercourse in the first place can be comforted and in many cases reversed, but only with practice and time. Practice and time that are worth taking, when the result is the kind of sexual intimacy you want.

Picture a young athlete. She is powerful, flexible, supple, and graceful. She practices her sport every morning and night. Then she graduates, gets a desk job, has a couple of kids, spends nearly every waking hour sitting at her desk or in her minivan, carpooling. Her fitness slowly drains away.

One day, she decides to get back into shape. If she tries to complete a workout at the level she did when she was in peak condition, she will get hurt. No doubt about it. She knows, or will soon realize, that she must start slowly. She'll get her fitness back, but only if she works within her comfort zone. When things start to hurt, she needs to back off. Keep moving, but slow down, decrease the intensity.

Please approach your new sexual aids, your vibrator of course, your vaginal dilators, especially, with this same understanding. Pushing too hard, going too fast, will hurt you. You are trying to restore pleasure, and I recommend letting comfort and pleasure be your guide.

As always, if the pain just won't resolve, do discuss it with your doctors. Finding the real reason for the pain is the fastest way to resolve it.

Meantime, put the box down. Have a healthy dinner. Take a nice bath. Relax. Then begin, slowly.

QUESTIONS... AND ANSWERS

Q: Why are orgasms different and more elusive now?

If you've missed periods, you are perimenopausal. It's likely that you are experiencing symptoms of less circulating estrogen. Hot flashes are the most common symptom from that, but the way we experience sex changes too. Medications taken for other conditions can compound the issue.

It is not unusual for orgasms to differ in sensation as a reflection of differing stimulation. Using a warming lubricant may help with arousal, or considering localized (vaginal) estrogen could also help. To help with arousal with a partner, you can introduce new techniques or bonding behaviors. With a partner or on your own, you might experiment with erotica—either books or DVDs. You may want to use a vibrator, or if you've been using one and it doesn't seem to be helping any more, consider one that offers more stimulation. We look specifically for more powerful vibrators that more effectively deliver the stimulation midlife women need. A patient told me recently that she hadn't had an orgasm in years, but with their new, stronger vibrator, she can!

Welcome to this new phase of sexual life!

Q: Will I ever orgasm?

You may be among the 4 percent who won't experience orgasm—who, for some reason, simply can't, under any circumstances. It's more likely that you're among the 96 percent who can. When a woman tells me she's not sure if she's experienced orgasm, I say she probably hasn't; it's fairly obvious when it happens.

Most women need direct clitoral stimulation to reach orgasm; what we see so often in movies, of partners climaxing together through intercourse alone, is rare in real life. Beyond that, there's plenty of variation: Some women may need an hour of clitoral stimulation; others may experience orgasm through brief nipple stimulation.

I recommend that each woman know her own clitoris, because degrees and types of pleasurable stimulation vary among us. Vibrators are very effective in stimulating the clitoris, and spending time yourself, exploring in a relaxed environment, will help you advise your partner on what feels good. Soothing or arousing music or a sexy scene from a movie can help, too.

When you're ready to go further, you can try internal stimulation, which leads to orgasm for about 30 percent of us. A vibrator like the Gigi2 can be used both externally and internally, so you can place it in the vagina (use a lubricant to be sure you're comfortable) and see what happens.

While chances are good (about 96 percent good!), there's no guarantee of orgasm. And because being focused only on orgasm can actually inhibit your ability to experience it, I hope you'll enjoy the intimacy and other sensations along the way!

Q: Could I be too stressed to orgasm?

You say that you're both excited and anxious about being with your partner, but that you're tense with him and haven't experienced this before. Let me first say that there's no magic pill that will solve this problem.

For women, sharing sexual intimacy requires the ultimate in trusting, giving, and sharing. This emotional component is just one part of a complex whole for women, but it's the place I'd start. I'm curious about whether you're tense with this partner in situations outside the bedroom, and whether you've been able to express your concern. It would be helpful it it's a problem you're looking to solve together rather than a "performance anxiety" issue for you alone. Being anxious about being able to experience orgasm only makes it more difficult!

You might consider seeing a therapist with a focus in sexuality to be sure that you're clear on the emotions and feelings you're experiencing.

If there is no emotional barrier to address, I've recommended Viagra or a very low dose of testosterone for women who have lost orgasm or intensity; both of these drugs are prescribed "off label," which means they're FDA-approved for another use.

I wonder whether you're able to experience orgasm with self-stimulation; if you haven't tried, I encourage you to. A vibrator used either alone or with your partner may provide the increased sensation you need. And if you're able to orgasm alone, you may learn some things about your response that you could share with your partner.

Sex is often complicated, with multiple interdependent components; it doesn't help that our bodies change as we gain years! Please do look to a therapist for any emotional considerations; if physical considerations remain, a health care provider knowledgeable about menopause can help you evaluate options. Most women in my practice are able to reclaim this part of their pleasure!

Q: How can I increase our success using a vibrator?

I'm glad to hear that a vibrator has been helpful to you! Women our age often need extra stimulation for arousal and orgasm, and many find that a vibrator provides just what they need. If you're looking for more, here are some things you might consider:

- » A stronger motor: Not all vibrators are created equal. Check for motor strength, because it really does matter to midlife women: a stronger motor means more stimulation. You can also check for the number of pulse patterns offered; there's nothing magic about them, but they make experimentation easier.

- » Get versatile: If you've started with an external clitoral vibrator, you might want to try a vibrator that can be used inside the vagina, too.

- » Size differs: You'll notice I didn't say that size matters, but different sizes do offer different sensations. One might have a two-inch diameter, for example, as compared to an inch for another; vibrators also vary in length.

Finally, stay playful and stay connected to your partner when you're being intimate. While vibrators are great as both tools and toys, especially for us as women, the emotional connection is arousing, too!

Q: Are my tissues shrinking down there?

What you ask about specifically is your clitoris, which, along with other genital tissues, does typically shrink with the loss of estrogen—whether through menopause or some other medical event. Because you're under 40, which is young for what you're describing, I'd encourage you to express your concern to your health care provider and have a thorough pelvic exam. The exam will be helpful in finding out whether there's another vulvar condition causing the tissue changes—or whether you're experiencing normal changes.

As we lose estrogen, we do face something of a "use it or lose it" proposition. That is, circulation and stimulation keep our genital tissues healthier; left to their own devices, they'll atrophy. If you don't have a partner right now, a vibrator is a great choice to provide stimulation and increased blood supply to the area. Maintaining your health means you'll be ready for intimacy when—just when you least expect it—a relationship emerges!

Q: Why do my Kegel exercise balls slide out?

The exercise balls slide out because the muscles of the pelvic floor are weak. Contracting and working the pelvic floor muscles will make them stronger, and they'll keep the exercise balls in place longer.

Start slowly: You might leave the balls in only a short time, keeping your pelvic floor muscles contracted to hold them in place. (Specific how-to instructions are on our website.) Depending on how much muscle strength you have, you may need to start while sitting or lying down rather than standing.

As with other muscles, it will take weeks to build strength in those muscles, but it definitely happens! Exercise balls or other Kegel tools help by making it easier to tell that you're flexing the right muscles. And the payoff is big—not only does a strong pelvic floor counter incontinence and hold your organs in place, it can also strengthen orgasm.

Q: Will Kegel exercises help me recover from pelvic floor damage from trauma?

It sounds like you could benefit from a really good pelvic floor physical therapist. While many physical therapists have some training with the pelvic floor, there are only a few with that specialty. Find out who that person is in your community and ask for a referral to him or her.

Physical therapists will have tools that help them determine the strength of the muscles, which helps them make an informed plan for properly improving the tone; Kegel exercises are just one tool in that process. Sometimes after a trauma there is muscle spasm; part of the therapy may be training certain muscles to relax.

It's a good approach to see how far you can get with exercise and therapy before you consider reconstructive surgery. Good luck with your continued recovery from your accident!

CHAPTER SIX

THE HORMONE CONUNDRUM

ONE TEST WHERE GRADES DON'T COUNT

Many of the women I see in my office would like a black and white answer: Where, exactly, are they on the path to menopause? Unfortunately, I can't really give them a solid answer, and here's why.

Perimenopause—that period (no pun intended!) between regular menstruation and menopause—isn't a steady progression. It's more like two steps forward, one step back. Sometimes, one step forward, two steps back. You may have some signs along the way, like moodiness, insomnia, irregular periods, hot flashes, lack of interest in sex, or vaginal dryness.

Sometimes FSH tests are used to help fill in the picture, providing one more data point. I don't often recommend these tests, though, because although the tests are accurate at that moment on that day, they can be wildly misleading—unless you're not yet in perimenopause (in which case the test can point to other issues) or you're in menopause—which you already know because you're not menstruating.

Here's what's happening with FSH (follicle stimulating hormone): The pituitary gland sends out FSH to tell the ovaries to make estrogen, which helps eggs grow (stimulating follicles!) and thickens the uterine lining. The pituitary gland acts like a thermostat: if it senses estrogen production is low, it "kicks on" and releases more FSH.

Chapter Six: The Hormone Conundrum

But as I said, the path to menopause is not a straight one; most women have erratic periods before menopause. So even if you are 52 and have every other symptom of perimenopause, if you take the test during the one time in six months you happened to ovulate, your FSH levels would suggest you're not menopausal. Lifestyle-related factors like stress and smoking also affect FSH levels, making them even less helpful.

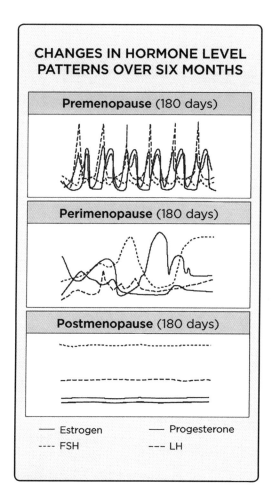

Check out the graphic to see the kind of unpredictability that's typical. The first graph shows regular hormonal fluctuation when you're having regular cycles. The second graph shows how wildly all four hormones may vary over six months. The last graph shows that a consistently high level of FSH accompanies menopause. But, again, if you're not having periods, you don't need a hormone test—either from a doctor or an at-home saliva test—to tell you you're menopausal. (If, by the way, you've had a hysterectomy, endometrial ablation, or another procedure that's eliminated periods but you still have ovaries, you have the same unpredictability in hormone levels. Charting your symptoms for a few months may be the most helpful approach.)

I understand that the ambiguity of perimenopause bothers some women. As a physician with a pretty good understanding of all the pieces at play, maybe I find it too easy to recommend that women tune in to their bodies and take it a month at a time.

MAKE YOUR OWN LOVE POTION

"I just want to want sex again."

I can't tell you how many of my patients have expressed—in one way or another—this simple desire for the desire they experienced in their 20s and 30s, when their bodies were flooded with procreative hormones.

Wouldn't it be great if I could mix up a love potion to send home with them and to share with you here? Some powerful concoction of roots and herbs perhaps, a magic elixir guaranteed to bring it all back?

Well, here's the next best thing. A recipe you can use to produce your own personal, all-natural love potion. For free.

Oxytocin, a hormone produced by the pituitary gland, has long been recognized for its role in childbirth and lactation and mother/child bonding. Women in labor are sometimes given a synthetic oxytocin to stimulate contractions. And mothers and babies both experience the pleasurable effects—calmness, trust, contentment—of the natural oxytocin that is released into their brains and blood streams during breast-feeding.

Recently though, research has been identifying the significant effects that "the cuddle hormone" have on men as well as women—and on their desire for (and enjoyment of) sex that isn't about making babies.

Both men and women experience rising oxytocin levels in response to being touched anywhere on their bodies. The effects promote a bond of closeness that increases sexual receptiveness—and the desire for even more touching. Even more touching leads to even more oxytocin which leads to even more arousal and even more desire for even more touching. Isn't it beautiful how that works?

There's more: high levels of oxytocin cause nerves in the genitals to fire spontaneously, triggering powerful orgasms. And during orgasm the body releases—you guessed it—more oxytocin. (Which, as it turns out, is good for you in all kinds of ways. Research indicates that oxytocin helps people sleep better, enhances feelings of well being, and counteracts the stress hormone, cortisol.)

The best thing about this amazing hormone for women our age is that — unlike estrogen and other sex hormones — you can make it yourself. Caressing your partner, enjoying a massage, bringing yourself to orgasm are all ways to get more oxytocin into your life. In fact, many women find that self-pleasuring is the best way to boost a sagging libido. More orgasms = more oxytocin = more desire.

You *can* get this wonderful pleasure cycle up and running!

E IS FOR ESTROGEN

Estrogen is the queen of hormones. From our brains to our bones to our bottoms, estrogen keeps our systems regulated, lubricated, elastic, and running smoothly. Estrogen doesn't just trigger sexual development in our breasts, uterus, vagina, and ovaries (although it does that, too), but it also regulates the production of cholesterol in our liver; it affects mood and body temperature from the brain; it protects against loss of bone density; and it keeps our sexual organs responsive and functional.

Estrogen is actually a category—a group composed of three chemically similar hormones. Estrone and estradiol are mostly produced in the ovaries, adrenal glands, and fatty tissue of all female mammals. Estriol is produced by the placenta during pregnancy. These estrogens circulate in the bloodstream and bind to receptors located throughout our bodies.

Not surprisingly, most of those estrogen receptors are located in the vulva, vagina, urethra, and the neck of the bladder, and that's why we talk about estrogen so much at MiddlesexMD. It's the critical hormone that keeps our sexual apparatus healthy and functional.

Before menopause, a healthy vagina has

- » thick, moist "skin," or epithelium

- » tissues with many folds (rugations) that allow the vagina to expand and become roomier

- » differentiated layers of cells—superficial and intermediate

- » secretions from the vaginal walls and cervix that help maintain a slightly acidic pH balance

- » an increase in blood flow and lubricating secretions during sexual arousal

- » toned pelvic floor muscles that help to hold our internal organs in place

So it's easy to see that when our estrogen levels drop dramatically during menopause, virtually all of us will experience significant change to our vulvovaginal tissue. The umbrella term for that change is "vulvovaginal atrophy." Here's what happens to our genital area when we lose estrogen:

- » the epithelium becomes pale, thin, and more likely to tear

- » the vagina shortens and narrows

- » vaginal walls lose rugations (those folds or pleats) and become smooth

- » cells become less differentiated—there are more intermediate and fewer superficial cells

- » the vagina becomes dry without secretions to maintain a good pH balance or to lubricate during sex

- » the vulva shrinks and pubic hair thins

» the pelvic floor loses muscle tone, so organs relax and sometimes sag (prolapse)

It's not a pretty list, but it's our new, postmenopausal normal. Vaginal atrophy can bring more frequent vaginal and urinary tract infections as well as more painful sex. And since painful sex usually means less sex, both our relationship and our quality of life can suffer.

Fortunately, there are simple and effective ways to ease the effect of estrogen loss. These include using moisturizers and lubricants or topical estrogen products, doing our kegels, and talking to our doctors about vulvovaginal changes.

Losing estrogen and its beneficial effects is inevitable as we grow older, but losing function, sexual or otherwise, isn't. Sex—and life—can be just as enjoyable. They just take more maintenance now.

ESTROGEN WHERE IT'S NEEDED

Okay, so you've tried everything. You regularly use a good, natural moisturizer, plus a lubricant during sex. No soaps, sprays, scents, dyes, or synthetic underwear ever touch your bottom. You're the queen of vaginal hygiene. And still you're troubled by dry, itching, or inflamed genitals and painful penetration.

What now?

Talk to your doctor about using a localized estrogen product for your vagina. These medicines deliver low dosages of estrogen right where it's needed: the vagina and vulva. Not only is localized estrogen medication very effective at relieving the discomfort of vaginal inflammation or atrophy, but it also restores natural vaginal lubrication and elasticity. In fact, while it won't relieve other menopausal symptoms—like hot flashes—low-dosage vaginal estrogen is sometimes more effective in relieving menopausal genital problems than systemic hormone replacement therapies (HRT). Moreover, the dosages are so low, the side effects and complications so negligible, it is often used by breast cancer survivors.

Vaginal estrogen comes in several forms: a cream (used twice a week), or slow-release tablets (used twice a week), or a ring (which needs to be replaced every three months). Don't, however, confuse the Estring vaginal ring with Femring, which is the high-dosage HRT in a vaginal ring form. (Confusing? It can be.) Your doctor will tailor the amount and frequency of application for the maximum effect at the lowest possible dose. It may also take several weeks for treatment to become fully effective.

A few precautions:

» Avoid applying your estrogen cream right before intercourse, since your partner can absorb it through his penis. Estrogen rings and tablets are meant to stay in place and don't have this effect.

» Continue to use non-hormonal lubricants and moisturizers if necessary.

» Have regular vaginal intercourse to augment natural lubrication and a healthy vagina.

While localized estrogen may not be the first line of defense against the unpleasant genital changes related to menopause, it's an important option when simpler methods (like vaginal lubricants or moisturizers) fail.

TESTOSTERONE: NOT FOR MEN ONLY

Testosterone, of course, is the hormone that makes guys hairy, muscular, and sexual. But testosterone isn't only for guys. Women produce it, too, but at much lower levels, and for us, the effects are less linear and more subtle: More testosterone doesn't necessarily mean more libido. Yet, in many studies, a little touch of testosterone has been strongly linked to a better sex life for women.

So, what's the big deal about testosterone, anyway? What's its role in women's sexuality, and what are the pros and cons of testosterone therapy for women?

First, a refresher: The most common cause of pain with intercourse for the peri-menopausal and menopausal woman is vaginal dryness that comes from the absence of estrogen—in medical terms, vaginal atrophy. The solutions are to restore vaginal estrogen (available by prescription) or restore moisture with regular use of non-hormonal, over the counter vaginal moisturizers.

So while estrogen is primary, we also produce testosterone—mainly in our ovaries, and only at about one-tenth the level as in men. Testosterone levels peak in our 20s and early 30s and steadily decline until, surprise!, we've lost about 80 percent of our testosterone-producing power after menopause. Women whose ovaries are removed are also cast immediately into "surgically induced menopause." While we may still be sexual creatures, we're no longer procreative creatures, so the hormonal stream is reduced to a trickle.

Enter testosterone therapy. Testosterone may be one rabbit in the bag of tricks that addresses the single biggest sexual complaint in women: lack of interest. Testosterone has been called the "hormone of desire" for women. "Women need estrogen for lubrication and comfort during sex. But they need testosterone to feel desire in the first place," according to author and "Today" show correspondent Judith Reichman in a 2005 *Washington Post* article. In many studies over the years, replacing testosterone has been linked to greater sexual desire, more intense orgasm, and improved sexual performance in women. There's evidence that it might also improve muscle tone and increase energy levels and mental acuity.

Yet, it's still only available "off-label," meaning that there's no pharmaceutical brand approved by the Food and Drug Administration (FDA). Testosterone can be prescribed by using the male FDA-approved products, at significantly lesser dosing regimens, or by compounding at pharmacies. Testosterone, in natural or synthetic form, is available in long-lasting injections, pellets, patches, and transdermal creams or gels. Oral testosterone or testosterone pills are not recommended because they are metabolized by the liver and there may be possible changes that result from that.

Testosterone therapy remains controversial. Unlike in men, there's no direct relationship between libido and blood testosterone levels in women. A woman can have a good sex drive with low testosterone or no interest in sex with high testosterone levels. Additionally, appropriate levels of testosterone for women have been hard to establish since we produce so little of it. Measuring testosterone levels in women is difficult, because of the very low levels and other factors that affect the circulating testosterone. The use of testosterone in women is usually well-tolerated but side effects may include acne and unwanted hair growth. The phase III clinical trials for testosterone use in women appear as though testosterone use in women is safe, but the FDA has not approved the product.

Before beginning testosterone therapy, it's important to address other causes of loss of libido, such as depression, medications, painful intercourse, lack of emotional intimacy, or chronic stress. But, if lack of interest in sex or the inability to experience orgasm continues to be a problem for you or in your relationship, testosterone therapy might be something to explore with your health care provider.

BEYOND THE HEADLINES: EVALUATING HRT RISKS

A magazine in my waiting room cites a study that suggests 40 ounces of caffeinated coffee a day to prevent memory loss. The downside, of course, is that you may not sleep at night—which would certainly interfere with my brain function! You may have heart palpitations. And you may become dehydrated. As with any decision about your health, there are trade-offs and implications to consider.

That's the message I'm sharing with patients who have more anxiety about hormone options after a report from the Women's Health Initiative (WHI) linked hormone therapy to breast cancer. Complexities and trade-offs don't make good headlines, but we need to think them through to make decisions about our own health.

Here are a few of the things beyond the headlines I'd like women to consider before ruling out any kind of hormone therapy:

Every death from breast cancer is, of course, tragic. Too many women are fighting this disease. But for context, the increased risk the WHI points to is 1 in 10,000. According to the National Cancer Institute,

12.2 percent of American women will be diagnosed with breast cancer at some point in their lives.

The data reviewed by the WHI was of a study using a particular combination of synthetic hormones: estrogen plus progesterone. What's underreported is that there was a decrease of 23 percent in breast cancer risk with estrogen alone, and that the study did not compare other formulations of hormones.

The age at which menopause happens plays a part in breast cancer risk. The risk from hormone therapy described in the study is roughly the same as the increased risk that happens naturally if a woman's menopause happens five years later—because of the longer exposure to her own natural estrogen and progesterone.

Obesity is a risk factor I wish got more attention: Women who are 20 pounds or more overweight when perimenopausal are twice as likely to develop breast cancer after menopause, and nearly half of breast cancer patients are obese (nearly half of U.S. citizens, too). Fat tissue produces estrogen (estrone), which gives an obese menopausal woman higher estrogen levels than women of healthy weight.

Quality of life counts, too, in evaluating risk, as a friend realized when she found her 80-year-old mother up a tree picking apples. My own mother would have benefited from the bone health that hormone therapy can provide. She had a hip fracture and replacement in her 50s and didn't walk again. My bone health, on the other hand, is still good, partly as a result of careful hormone therapy.

If your menopause symptoms make you miserable, I'd encourage you to consider all of the options open to you. Consider your entire health picture, including your medical history, your weight, and how active you are. A good menopause care provider can help you explore your options and risks, and, if it's appropriate for you, prescribe the lowest effective level of the fewest possible hormones for a period of time to help you through the symptoms that are keeping you from living the life you'd like.

BIOIDENTICAL HORMONES: FLAP? OR NO FLAP?

Suzanne Somers touts them in her bestselling book, *Ageless: The Naked Truth about Bioidentical Hormones*. Oprah promotes their use. On the other hand, the Harvard Medical School, the North American Menopause Society, and the Endocrine Society take a more cautionary position toward *compounded* bioidentical hormones. And I find that many of my patients are just confused.

So what *are* bioidentical hormones and what's all the controversy surrounding them?

We talk a lot at MiddlesexMD about the importance of estrogen to vaginal health and sexual function. We've also discussed various options for replacing estrogen and enhancing vaginal comfort. And we explored the latest thinking about hormone replacement therapy (HRT).

In a nutshell, estrogen is critical to sexual comfort and function, and that's the hormone we lose during menopause. Most therapies revolve around replacing estrogen to treat menopausal symptoms.

For many years, Premarin was the estrogen replacement of choice. This is a synthetic estrogen made from the urine of pregnant mares, which, according to the *Harvard Women's Health Watch*, "contains a mix of estrogens (some unique to horses), steroids, and various other substances."

Bioidentical hormones, on the other hand, are defined by the Endocrine Society as "compounds that have exactly the same chemical and molecular structure as hormones that are produced in the human body." Bioidentical hormones are usually extracted from plant sources.

Pharmaceutical companies manufacture many brands of bioidentical estrogens, such as Vivelle, Elestrin, Divigel, Evamist and one brand of bioidentical progesterone (Prometrium). These are FDA-approved bioidentical hormones. About 95 percent of my patients who take supplementary hormones are on these FDA-approved bioidentical hormones.

Chapter Six: The Hormone Conundrum

All hormones, whether they are synthetic or bioidentical, are labeled with the black-box warnings mandated since the massive Women's Health Initiative study linked slightly higher rates of breast cancer, blood clots, and heart disease to hormone replacement therapy.

So far, so good.

Confusion enters in when bioidentical hormones are custom-compounded by pharmacies. Sometimes there are good reasons for a doctor to prescribe a custom-compounded hormone, if a patient is allergic to some agent in the FDA-approved hormones, for example, or if her dosage can be lower than those produced by pharmaceutical companies.

But hormones made by custom compounders aren't subject to FDA oversight, nor must they adhere to FDA-approved processes. These custom hormones don't come with black-box warnings because they don't fall under the FDA umbrella.

In actual practice, there may not be that much difference between custom hormones and FDA-approved hormones. According to the *Harvard Women's Health Watch*, in a 2001 random test of 37 hormone products from 12 compounding pharmacies, almost one-quarter (24 percent) were less potent than prescribed, while 2 percent of FDA-approved products were less potent.

The other problem with custom compounds is cost. Health insurance usually doesn't cover them, so the regimen gets expensive very quickly.

While custom compounds may be a helpful option for some women, the controversy surrounds the claims about them made by celebrities like Suzanne Somers and even by some clinicians.

In the introduction to her book, Somers writes, "This new approach to health [bioidentical hormone replacement therapy] gives you back your lean body, shining hair, and thick skin, provided you are eating correctly and exercising in moderation. This new medicine allows your brain to work perfectly and offers the greatest defense against cancer, heart attack, and Alzheimer's disease. Don't you want that?"

Well, who wouldn't? But like most claims that sounds too good to be true, so is this one.

The truth is that bioidentical compounds, no matter how "natural and safe" they may sound, are still drugs. There's no scientific evidence that their effect is any different than synthetic hormones. Also, because hormonal levels vary from day to day, even from hour to hour, attempting to customize hormonal treatments is tricky business. "There's no stable 'normal' value at all for salivary or blood levels of these hormones or levels that correlate with symptoms," says the *Harvard Women's Health Watch*.

The current medical advice is to take the lowest possible dosage of any hormone—synthetic or bioidentical—for the shortest period of time to alleviate menopausal symptoms. There is, unfortunately, no way to turn back the clock—"natural" or otherwise. In the meantime, the hormones that work for a woman can significantly improve her quality of life.

QUESTIONS... AND ANSWERS

Q: I quit the pill and tested mid-menopause in one month; now sex hurts. Suggestions?

Isn't it amazing how quickly things can change? You say you were tested as being mid-menopause. Blood work is accurate at assessing ovarian function on the day you're tested, but it is miserable in predicting what may happen in the next weeks or months. An FSH level may come back 40 (suggesting menopause) on one day, but you may ovulate 6 weeks from now and have an FSH at 8. It's really only over time that you really can better understand if this is the 'new norm' or transient. Perimenopause is known to have fluctuating symptoms; once in menopause, most women's symptoms are more predictable.

To make sex comfortable again, I would start with a lubricant. I would try a water-based lube like Carrageenan or Yes. If using a lube makes you comfortable and doesn't irritate the area, that can be a great, simple solution for now.

A warming lube can add some additional sensation for arousal and make orgasm somewhat stronger. Occasionally the warming lubes can be irritating if the area is sensitive, which is why I'd start with a non-stimulating water-based lube; then test a small amount of the warming lube to see if it works for you!

Good luck! I know you can have satisfying sex again.

Q: Can I use a moisturizer with my localized hormone cream?

Absolutely you can, and I often recommend that women use both. Both vaginal estrogen creams–like Estrace–and vaginal moisturizers–like Replens–are typically used twice a week.

Because each needs to be absorbed and, frankly, because it might otherwise be a little messy, I recommend that you alternate application. You might, for example, use the Estrace on Monday and Thursday and the Replens on Tuesday and Friday.

Glad you're taking care of yourself!

Q: My libido is higher than ever! Will it last? Should I be concerned?

When you're in perimenopause, we say that your hormone levels are, in general, declining. While they are declining "in general," it's likely that your levels of estrogen and progesterone are fluctuating erratically from day to day. Testosterone is usually more steady, not particularly fluctuating day to day or month to month. As a result, the mix of hormones changes, and for some women testosterone seems to play a more dominant role; one effect of testosterone is enhanced libido (it's sometimes considered as part of therapy to restore sexual function).

This may explain what you are experiencing. You asked whether you should be tested for hormone levels. While it's possible to measure hormone levels, and those measurements are accurate, the levels are accurate only for that hour or day and are not particularly helpful to predict what to plan on in the upcoming days or months.

I would say, enjoy the current state! I hope this is your 'new norm.'

Q: Is an estrogen ring or cream a better option?

Vaginal estrogen is the most effective treatment for vaginal atrophy and its symptoms: dryness, itching, irritation, pain with intercourse. There are three low-dose, localized (without systemic absorption) estrogen options: the vaginal ring (Estring), vaginal tablets (Vagifem), and vaginal creams (Premarin and Estrace). I prefer the ring and tablets, because the cream is messy to use and the absorption is somewhat more variable. Studies confirm there is no significant or noted changes in circulating blood estradiol levels with the ring and tablet; the creams are more variable and therefore more likely to have transient elevations in estradiol levels. I have many breast cancer patients who use these methods.

There is also now a non-estrogen option to treat dyspareunia (pain with intercourse), that arises because of the absence of estrogen in menopause. The new product is Osphena, it is dosed orally and taken daily and is very effective treatment for this condition.

Women who are candidates for vaginal estrogen often also consider over-the-counter lubricants and moisturizers. Lubricants make sex more comfortable in the moment, but don't improve or prevent the progression of the atrophy. Vaginal moisturizers give more lasting comfort. Used independent of sex on a continuous basis, usually two times a week, they can help restore moisture to the tissues. The moisturizers can also help restore a more healthy pH, promote elimination of dead cells, and increase moisture in the tissues.

If there are multiple menopausal symptoms, which may include vaginal dryness, systemic estrogen (like Vivelle) might be considered, weighing all health factors in the decision.

Q: What's the connection between HRT and cancer of the endometrium?

A definition first: The endometrium is the mucous membrane that lines the uterus. For women who have had hysterectomies, the endometrium is not an issue in planning hormone therapy (HT).

For others, the endometrium is a "target tissue" (like many others) for estrogen and progesterone. During our reproductive years, those hormones signaled the lining of the uterus to thicken (proliferative endometrium influenced by estrogen) and then to shed (secretory endometrium influenced by progesterone), over and over in our menstrual cycle.

Endometrial cancer is a well-recognized consequence of "unopposed estrogen," a continual message to proliferate and thicken without the proper "opposing" influence of progesterone. Nearly all endometrial cancers will be "estrogen influenced."

When we plan HT for a woman in menopause with a uterus, we must balance estrogen and progesterone. (And, in fact, for a woman in reproductive years who doesn't ovulate, which typically triggers progesterone, we'll compensate with progesterone therapy.)

As with most cancers, there are factors we can't always explain. Obesity, however, is the most common risk factor; in fact, obese women are at higher risk than their friends on HT including both estrogen and progesterone. Fat (adipose) tissue produces estrone, an estrogen that is very weak but does influence the endometrium. Sometimes we biopsy obese women and find "precancer" of the endometrium; part of our treatment is progesterone in an effort to reduce their cancer risk.

Just one more reason, I'm afraid, to make healthy habits a priority—and to work with your health care provider for HT that takes your health history and priorities into account.

CHAPTER SEVEN

HEALTH REALITIES AND HOPE

I WILL OVERCOME

Of course, we'd all love to enjoy good health and great sex until the day we die peacefully in our sleep. While we can control many aspects of our health, sometimes we just draw the short straw. Conditions like arthritis, heart disease, cancer, and lung problems can change our lives, our self-image, our relationships, what we're capable of doing, and our experience of the world.

And without attention, our sex life with all its pleasure, tenderness, and intimacy can become collateral damage in the wake of illness.

It doesn't have to be this way. In fact, it's a shame to forgo that shared pleasure and special bond just when it's most needed. Despite the challenges, there's no need to lay aside your sexual self in the face of health issues. And there's every reason to make the effort to reinvent and reinvigorate the way you experience and express sex in your relationship.

In fact, illness could challenge you to communicate in ways you never did before. You might learn to enjoy the moment and be grateful for what's left—or at least take less for granted. And the physical limitations of illness could lead you and your partner to become more sexually aware, patient, and experimental than ever before.

At a conference of the International Society for the Study of Women's Sexual Health (ISSWSH), a presentation on sexual rights reminded me of the many patients who try so hard to maintain normal lives in the face of life-changing health issues. This declaration of sexual rights is derived from a more extensive document first articulated by the IPPF. Here are the sexual rights as they relate to you—mature women who are redefining their lives, including their sexual lives, in the face of illness. You have the right to

» the highest level of sexual health you can attain

» information related to sexual health

» decide whether or not to be sexually active

» consensual sexual relations that are free from abuse

» a satisfying and pleasurable sex life

So, in the spirit of these sexual rights, I'll explore some health conditions that can make sex—and life—challenging and suggest ways that might help bring back the joy of sex again. With education and commitment, you can still enjoy the highest level of sexual health possible. Despite limitations, you can express your sexual self with confidence and vitality.

SEX AND ARTHRITIS: A NEW KIND OF REACH

As we age, few of us escape periodic (or not-so-periodic) joint pain. While it may be possible to work around occasional pain and stiffness in a knee or elbow, when arthritis is constantly painful and potentially debilitating, everyday activities become newly challenging.

When replacing the cap on the toothpaste requires effort, having intercourse with our partner may seem like reaching for the moon. But just as we find new ways to replace caps and button blouses, we can reach for new ways to give and receive sexual pleasure. This may demand effort, experimentation, and communication, but the effort may also pay off in a deeper and more satisfying level of intimacy.

Here's what leading rheumatologists and orthopedists have to say:

BE COMPASSIONATE with yourself and your partner. Arthritis is painful, and pain is exhausting. Further, medications for arthritis may cause vaginal dryness and fatigue. Rest, patience, and vaginal lubricants can help.

COMMUNICATE. Your partner needs to understand the emotional and physical changes you're experiencing, and you need to understand how your partner feels. Maybe you don't feel sexy. Maybe your partner is afraid of hurting you during intercourse. It may help to begin the dialog in front of a doctor or other professional who can direct the conversation and also suggest possible remedies. Keep in mind that silence often looks a lot like rejection.

PLAN AHEAD. Like other activities, a vital sex life will take more planning.

- » Schedule a "sex date" for a time of day when you tend to feel good.
- » Rest during the day—take a nap and avoid overexertion.
- » Take pain meds when they're likely to be effective, about half an hour before your "date."
- » Enjoy a warm bath (maybe with your partner) or use an electric blanket or heating pad to relax joints.
- » Do range-of-motion exercises to increase flexibility.
- » Look forward to the special time. Wear something sexy.

EXPERIMENT. Good sex leaves you and your partner feeling intimate, connected, and sexually satisfied, and there are many ways to skin this particular cat. Try new positions that take the pressure off painful areas and allow your partner to do more of the motion. Try using pillows for support or cushioning. Try massage or other loving touch. Oral sex or manual stimulation can be pleasurable. If your hands are affected, try using a vibrator on sensitive areas—the clitoris and the underside of the penis. Let your partner know what feels good—and what doesn't. In fact, agree upon a signal that will stop the action if you experience pain.

When you have arthritis, life happens at a different pace—more tortoise than hare. But we all know how *that* story ended. As long as you keep moving, you're winning.

SEX AND DEPRESSION

When a patient tells me that she no longer enjoys sex, one of first things I ask her is to tell me about something that she does enjoy.

If she isn't able to come up with a fairly quick answer, in my experience it's likely that depression is playing a part in her loss of libido.

Anhedonia—the inability to gain pleasure from normally pleasurable experiences — is a core clinical feature of depression. And because depression affects nearly twice as many women as men, and because recent studies suggest that midlife is a period of increased risk for depression in women, I am always on the alert when a patient mentions that she has stopped enjoying activities—like sex—that used to give her pleasure.

The cause-and-effect relationships between menopause and depression and between depression and loss of libido are complicated—to say the least!

Some studies suggest that changes in hormonal levels, such as those that occur during the transition to menopause, may trigger depression. The production of mood-enhancing neurotransmitters is boosted by estrogen. Lower levels of estrogen that accompany menopause can mess with the brain's chemical balance, leading to depression. Other biochemical changes that come with age, such as those that result from decreased thyroid function, have also been linked to the onset of depression.

But the pressures and stresses associated with midlife surely play a role as well. The loss of our youthful looks, of our reproductive and mothering roles, and sometimes even of our jobs or life partners—all make us vulnerable to depression as we move into and through our menopausal years.

Whatever the cause—and at whatever age—depression has a significant impact on sexual function and enjoyment. Nearly half of all women—and men—diagnosed with depression report that it interferes with their sexuality.

The good news: If depression is behind your loss of interest in and enjoyment of sex, there is an array of proven treatments to relieve the underlying cause and its symptoms. Your doctor can help identify and treat medical causes, such as thyroid problems. In some cases, hormone replacement therapy that elevates estrogen levels may be effective. Antidepressants that help correct chemical imbalances in the brain help many (although these may have their own sexual side-effects). Regular exercise, improved sleep habits, and dietary changes can help to counteract depression, and counseling and support groups are other options to explore.

Don't let depression drain the pleasure from your life. Talk to your doctor. See our website for more information on hormonal changes and therapeutic resources.

SEX AND BACK PAIN: A WORK-AROUND PRIMER

Long, long ago, when humankind first stood up on two feet, some bit of engineering seems to have gone missing. As a result, back pain is practically programmed into the human condition. The lucky ones may experience temporary pain from strained muscles, but for many, back pain can involve severe and constant pain from malfunctioning disks, nerve issues, bone issues, and a host of other maladies.

Unfortunately, nothing saps enjoyment and energy from life like pain. Whether intermittent or chronic, back pain can lay the sufferer, literally, flat on his or her back. Sex, obviously, becomes an early casualty. A 2008 survey found that most people who suffer from back pain have less sex, and they don't enjoy it much. They say the pain has affected their relationships, but they don't tend to talk about it either with their partners or their doctors. (And apparently, their doctors don't bring up the issue of sex, either.)

There are ways to work around this state of affairs, however, from communicating with your partner and your doctor to experimenting with positions that might make intercourse more comfortable. One doctor even says that sex can actually help ease back pain by "mobilizing 'stuck' segments in the spine" and by releasing "feel good" endorphins in the brain. Not to mention returning a sense of intimacy and normalcy to the relationship. So, nurturing a sense of intimacy in your most important relationship is probably worth working on, right?

We've beaten this drum before, but communication is critical. First, it's important to talk to your doctor. Do you have a diagnosis? Do you know what's causing your back pain? If pain, depression, or fear is affecting your sex life, your doctor may well have some advice, from changing the dosages of your medication to suggesting positions that might alleviate pain.

Second, talk to your partner. Chronic pain is hard to understand if you're not experiencing it. It feels like the "not now, dear, I have a headache" routine. It feels like rejection or at least avoidance.

If you've been avoiding sex, clear the air with your partner. You both need to express how you feel. Are you afraid that sex will hurt your back even more? That you're somehow "damaged goods"? Does the pain sap your energy? Do you feel depressed? Listen to your partner's fears and frustrations, too. If the conversation is too difficult, maybe you and your partner should discuss it with a therapist. The good news is that, with some courage and experimentation, intimacy and intercourse don't need to be held hostage to back pain.

TAKE IT SLOW. Prepare yourself. Take a warm bath to relax muscles. Plan your rendezvous for a time of day when you tend to feel good. Take your pain meds. Set the mood (candles, incense, music). Good sex is as much about the ambience as about acrobatics anyway.

Plan your positions. Depending on the type of back pain you experience, different positions will help ease your pain. Use firm pillows for support under the small of your back, under your neck or head, under your knees—wherever it feels comfortable.

Those with herniated discs tend to feel better when the spine is extended (arched). Use a pillow under your back for the missionary position or have your partner sit on a chair while you straddle. Both these positions tend to keep your back straight or slightly arched.

For those with spinal stenosis, on the other hand, slightly flexing (humping) the back feels better. Keep your knees pulled toward you in the missionary position or drape your legs over your partner's shoulders. Both positions keep the spine arched.

Try lying on your side. Or lie on the side of the bed with your legs dangling off the side. Just be sure you're well-supported on a firm surface. Use the pillows wherever you need more support. The rule of thumb is that the partner without the pain should do the work. Take it slow, and if something hurts, stop!

Do kegels. Besides strengthening your pelvic floor muscles, which is good for sex, this exercise also develops your core musculature, which is good for your back.

A highly recommended book specifically dealing with this issue is *Sex and Back Pain: Advice on Restoring Comfortable Sex Lost to Back Pain*, by physical therapist Lauren Andrew Hebert.

SEX AFTER HEART DISEASE: GOOD FOR THE BODY, GOOD FOR THE HEART

Heart disease is a sobering reminder of mortality. After a heart attack or surgery, you live with a new reality. Maybe you're faced with dietary restrictions or lifestyle changes or a new pharmaceutical regimen. Probably you're more conscious of your breathing and your heart rate. With all the preoccupations and adjustments that accompany heart disease, sex can become a low priority. Maybe you're afraid that intercourse will damage your newly fragile heart or actually trigger a heart attack. Or maybe it's hard even to be interested in sex.

Chapter Seven: Health Realities and Hope

After a heart attack, it's important to resume normal activities and to feel connected to people and life. What better way to feel vital and connected than to make love with your most intimate companion? Generally, the issues that stifle your sex life after a heart attack or surgery have to do with fear, depression, medication, and lack of communication with the doctor.

First, let's address the persistent myth that sex can cause a heart attack. Studies repeatedly show that, if you can walk up a flight of stairs or carry a 20-pound bag of groceries into the house, you're fit enough for sex. If you've passed the stress tests and are cleared to resume normal activity, what better activity than sex? Sure beats doing the laundry.

If you continue to worry, air your concerns with your doctor. An eye-opening study conducted at the University of Chicago revealed that doctors frequently neglect to talk with patients about their sex lives following a myocardial infarction, and that this tendency was particularly pronounced with female patients. (Less than half the men and less than one-third of women received instructions about sex when they were discharged from the hospital.) Patients who didn't receive guidance from their doctors about sex were less likely to be sexually active in the year following their heart attack. So if the doctor doesn't advise you about sex, please initiate the conversation yourself!

Depression commonly follows on the heels of heart disease, and women are more likely to become depressed than men. And both depression and many antidepressant drugs are likely to suppress sexual interest, leaving you between a rock and a hard place, sexually speaking. The good news is that depression after heart surgery or a heart attack usually resolves itself in about three months.

Other medications, such as beta-blockers that lower blood pressure and regulate heart rate, have also been linked with depression and sexual dysfunction. Again, your doctor may be able to adjust dosages or switch medication if necessary.

Finally, the good news is that sex is good for you emotionally and physically. It's like a gentle, pleasurable workout. And anything you can do to improve your overall health–exercising, losing weight, stopping smoking–will improve your heart health and, incidentally, the quality of your sexual life.

BREATHING PROBLEMS (COPD) AND SEX: TAKE MY BREATH AWAY

When you exercise, you need more oxygen. Sex is like a light exercise—you need more oxygen then, too. For people with chronic obstructive pulmonary disease (COPD), such as asthma, emphysema, or chronic bronchitis, that breathing space may be hard to come by. Further complicating the physical condition is the emotional fear of not being able to breathe.

Taken together, these emotional and physical limitations present an obstacle to the carefree sex of former days. But just as you develop new ways to accomplish other daily activities, you can continue to enjoy a fulfilling sex life. You just have to make adjustments. Such as:

STAY IN SHAPE. Heard this before? To enjoy the highest quality of life possible, you need to be as healthy as possible. This means to continue to exercise and to maintain a healthy weight. Discuss ways to improve your health with your doctor. See if there's a pulmonary rehab program in your area where you can learn safe ways to exercise. Your quality of life will be better, and so will the quality of your sex life.

PREPARE THE ENVIRONMENT. For those with allergies or lung conditions, the bedroom is the most important area to keep clean and allergen-free. That means no fragrances, smoke, pet dander, or dust. Keep the mattress and pillows enclosed in allergenic covers. Use a HEPA filter on the vacuum and consider using one in the room itself.

PREPARE YOURSELF. In order to enjoy these intimate encounters, psychological preparation is as important as physical preparation. Think about what you need to feel secure during sex. How can you communicate with your partner if you begin to feel breathless? What can you do to approach intercourse as a pleasurable act without anxiety?

Some physical preparation can also help you feel safe and comfortable. Keep your inhalers at the bedside. Take a puff or two of your short-acting bronchodilator about 15 minutes before having sex. If you use oxygen, keep it bedside as well. Add tube extensions to the nasal canula so you have more wiggle room. Wait a couple hours after a meal to have sex.

DO IT. Experiment with positions that take pressure off your chest—lying on your side or sitting on a chair, perhaps. Use pillows to help prop you up. Take it slow and easy—cuddling and touching are nice, too. Run a fan—cool air on your face can help ease breathing and diffuse any heat buildup in the area.

Use supplemental oxygen if you have to and stop if you get winded. Talk to your doctor about increasing the oxygen flow during sex.

Don't overlook the many alternative ways to give and receive pleasure. You can use manual stimulation, for example, or use a vibrator on the clitoris and the underside of the penis.

When normal activities consume more energy, and fatigue is the shadow at your elbow, making love may seem like climbing Everest. But just as you find ways to accomplish those mundane tasks, it will be even more rewarding to find new ways to make love.

SEX AND CANCER

> *"Not everything that is faced can be changed,*
> *but nothing can be changed until it is faced."*
> *–James Baldwin*

We've been hearing from many women who are receiving treatments for various forms of cancer: What about us, they ask. Post-menopause is one thing, but what about post-cancer treatment? Or mid-treatment? How do we maintain intimacy when we are going through chemo or radiation or when surgery has changed our bodies and the way we feel about them?

We sat down to discuss these very difficult questions with our colleague Mary Jo Rapini. Her practice gathers couples referred before, during, and after cancer treatment to talk about sexuality and intimacy and how to maintain physical expressions of love when we are sick.

Here's what Mary Jo told us:

I see lots of women with breast, ovarian, and uterine cancer in my practice. I ask to see her first, before meeting with the couple together. Women have a strong protective instinct; they will put up walls when they get sick, in part to protect themselves, but also to protect their loved ones, to avoid burdening them. I will coach her to share this crisis. That protective sense turns out to be too distancing. Whatever she is going through, whatever she decides for her course of treatment, the people who love her are in it with her. Their world is changing too, and it's important to respect that and bring them along on the journey, consult with them. It's important to have a team in this fight.

When a couple comes to me mid-treatment or post-treatment, they walk through the door with the goal to restore their sex life. The first thing I do is to slow them down, to hit the reset button. I give them a list of things to think about that goes like this:

1. Focus on the positive.

2. Take intercourse off the table until you have the energy for it, but don't stop thinking about sex. Don't stifle your own sexual thoughts out of guilt. Tell your partner, I still really desire you and wish I could make love to you.

3. Remember sex is more than intercourse.

4. Discuss your fears of the cancer.

5. Consider buying your partner something sexy or feminine that will help her feel like a woman.

6. Be a good listener and let her set the pace.

My focus for couples at this important time is to feel pleasure and relaxation first, before working on feeling excited. Excitement is exhausting, and exhaustion can lead to failure and frustration. I ask them to just flat out remove the goals of intercourse and orgasm from the picture. I promise we will get to these, eventually, but for now, let's not worry about it.

I had an aneurysm that nearly cost me my life. For me, orgasms changed a lot. For one thing, they made my head ache. With a clip on arteries in my brain, and my blood flow trying to figure out a new path—orgasm took a lot out of me. Sex didn't give me the energetic feeling I used to have. Instead, orgasms robbed me of energy for the rest of the day. A lot of my cancer patients tell me that intimacy tires them, so planning is important.

A recovering cancer patient has to plan how she will spend the little energy she has on home and health and relationships. This is a very important adjustment, especially if a couple has always enjoyed a spontaneous sex life in the past. Your chest may be a surgical site; chemotherapy and radiation may make you nauseous, bloated, and incredibly fatigued; it may induce menopause if you haven't already made that passage. Cancer survivors frequently experience depression as well. It's important to know that if you don't feel like sex for a period of time, you don't have to go there. Focus on getting well first.

Your partner is under a lot of pressure, too, and is probably struggling to find purchase on the slippery slope of this crisis, uncertain about how to support you, and how or when to approach the sticky wicket of sex. Your partner may be waiting for you to make the first move, or be afraid of hurting you.

I prescribe a lot of hand-holding and hugging. We know the importance of hugging now, how it builds and maintains bonds for us. Most men will tell me that when their partner is sick, this is what they miss more than anything. The worst thing people can do when they can't have sex is to withhold all touch. When a couple only touches as a precursor to sex, touch can be loaded with expectations, and we need to break through that. We need to experience touch as a pleasure in itself.

During treatment, during chemo and radiation, just take intercourse off the table, but replace it with lots and lots of touch. Hand holding, back scratching, feather-brushing, rubbing hair, petting. Have fun touching, kissing, necking, without the worry of failure. Just revel in closeness. Notice how your sensations may have changed--are your neck, shoulders, ears more sensitive than before the cancer?

Once you've gotten this connection really going, add water. Because water is relaxing. Shower together. Or take a bubble bath (but stay away from very strong scents). Light candles, bring in soft music. Focus on enjoying each other. Wash each other. Especially, wash each other's feet. When something feels especially good, say so.

When you are in treatment for cancer, self exploration is really important. Experiment with self touch, especially where you have had surgery. Touching helps you deal with grief of loss and letting go. If you have lost a breast, you need to feel that void and be able to grieve it.

Experts say that you don't have to "love your scars." If you're uncomfortable letting your partner see you naked, wear sexy lingerie. Whether to include your partner in this exploration is entirely your choice, but it can very helpful for both you and your partner to join in this exploration and support you in your grief.

With any kind of an illness, the ill person asks, "Who am I now?" A serious illness changes the self, sometimes just a bit, but often profoundly. And if one self in a couple changes, then it follows that the couple's sense of couplehood changes. Talk together about the changes you experience and notice.

A healthy partner often feels guilty about wanting sex; he knows a sick partner doesn't have energy for sex. The healthy partner is a caretaker and not a lover right now. Talking about that is very helpful and important. Getting a counselor to talk with both or either of you during this time of adjustment can be the best investment you've ever made.

If you are sick, don't underestimate your lover. We are all pretty good at putting our sexual needs on the shelf, as long as we feel loved. The most helpful way to show your love is through touch. Touching can

Chapter Seven: Health Realities and Hope

make talking more available. Some things you hate to tell your partner. But if you are touching them while you talk, there are moments when the communication is so authentic, you will find you can say anything. And that is the sound of real intimacy.

When a couple is referred to me, it's usually because the cancer part of their life is now under control. That is, they have their diagnosis, understand staging, and have been receiving treatments, with some evidence that treatments are working. Until that point, survival is the critical concern for most couples.

This time of diagnosis and sheer survival can actually bring couples closer—they realize that what they used to argue about is petty. On the other hand, really bad relationships will many times get worse. Women who are sick might ask themselves what they're doing, what happened in their relationship. When that's the case, my first step is figuring out the emotional environment. Where is this couple now, at this moment in time?

When we do come around to talking about intimacy in the relationship, my first concern is with pain. Painful sex is a really common problem for survivors. Low energy is another problem. People receiving treatments or recovering from extensive treatments have very low stores of energy.

Women recovering from surgery and radiation for any kind of cancer, including breast or uterine cancers, may be adjusting to new losses and scars that affect body image, sensation, mobility, or all three.

And while thinking about restoring sexuality may be pretty far from her mind, the truth is that reengaging with a lover has been shown to really help with recovery. Sex is very healthy—for our bodies and our minds—and a loving intimacy is certainly one of the best things we have to live for.

GET HELP. Your intimate life may have been perfect your whole lives, your relationship sound, your commitment to one another unshakable, but still a good counselor can give you things to think about, assignments and exercises that can help you to re-engage after harrowing course of treatment. Consider it a gift to yourselves, a reward for surviving.

PLANNING IS EVERYTHING. Spontaneous sex was great when you were teenagers, but now things are different. Intimacy is best now when it is anticipated and planned. Choose a day of the week when nothing much else is going on. Choose a time in that day when you are likely to have less pain. Be sure you have an hour of pain medication in your body before engaging in cuddling and caressing.

SET A NEW GOAL. Sexuality is often so goal-oriented we forget that sex is good for more than just orgasm. When orgasm is difficult to reach—for either of you—why not take it off the table and enjoy the benefits of sexual intimacy without it? Massaging erogenous zones is extremely pleasurable—provided there is no pain—whether we achieve orgasm or not. It still circulates blood, increases healthy hormone production, and helps couples bond to one another. Set a new goal: bonding and intimacy. Use that vibrator to make one another purr, and let purring be enough for a while.

BECOME A PROP MASTER. Pillows, pillows, pillows. If you spend any time in a hospital, you will notice that nurses really know how to use pillows to prop people into comfort in bed. Well, we can use them too, to prop us into comfortable positions for intimate caressing and lovemaking. We may not have needed them before surgeries or treatment, but may really need them now, when a slight change in position or angle may make a huge difference in comfort and painless lovemaking.

PATIENT EXPLORATION IS THE KEY. Most of us don't know how our bodies will respond to treatment. Our mileage varies. So patiently exploring how treatment may have changed our sense of touch and taste and smell, in addition to pain and pleasure—this takes time. Be a scientist about it. Experiment, experiment, with all the patience of a field biologist!

USE A LIGHT TOUCH. When we get chemo, our skin can become very sensitive. Chemo changes the epidermis of the skin. Our sense of touch shifts. That's where things like feathers, mitts, and lotions become so important as tools for exploration, because your body is different on chemo. Figuring out those changes is the work ahead for both of you.

Some of the chemos are so toxic any intercourse would be too rough on fragile tissues. That's a good time to think about a different form of expression, beyond intercourse. Find new ways to connect.

WETNESS NOW, MORE THAN EVER. Most women can't handle intercourse during treatment. Chemotherapy can be very drying, and our skin, our vaginal tissues, are just too fragile. But if you are going to try intercourse during treatment, lubrication is extremely important. Try a lube that has a trace of silicone. I especially like Liquid Silk for this purpose. A little bit of silicone can give that lube sticking power. Too much is hard for a dry vagina to clear on its own.

Slow down. Pretend you are new lovers, virgins, even. Go very slowly. Be prepared to relearn everything about to make love to each other. Kissing can change. Taste can change. Relax, take interest, explore, report, and learn.

AFTER CANCER: TAKE CARE OF YOUR VAGINA

Whether you were already menopausal or were abruptly deposited into menopause after treatment for your cancer, you're probably familiar with what happens to your vagina when you lose estrogen.

You may experience the burning, itching pain of thin, dry vaginal walls and fragile skin on your genitals. You don't lubricate like you used to, so sex can be difficult or painful. Or, if you're experiencing the muscle spasms of vaginismus, sex may be impossible. Less estrogen is a good thing for some cancer treatments, but it's darned tough on the vagina and, by extension, on your sex life as well.

So, while vaginal health is important for all women during menopause, it's critical for those undergoing cancer treatment. Your vagina and pelvic floor need a lot of TLC right now to stay comfortable and responsive. Fortunately, compared to the other things going on in your life, taking care of your bottom is usually straightforward and inexpensive. Besides, keeping your vagina in good shape might eliminate one problem area and allow you to stay in touch with your sexual self, too.

Consider this four-part approach to caring for your vagina and pelvic floor.

First, use vaginal moisturizers and lubricants.

Moisturizers are your first line of defense. These are non-hormonal, over-the-counter products that are intended to keep your vagina hydrated and to restore a more natural pH balance. They should be used two or three times a week, just as you'd moisturize any other part of your body.

Using moisturizers is important whether or not you're having intercourse. It should just be part of a regular health maintenance regimen.

Use lubricants liberally before intercourse, on sex toys such as vibrators, and any time you touch the delicate tissue on your genitalia. Also apply lubricant to your partner's penis.

At this point, keep your lubricants plain and simple—no scents or flavors; avoid warming lubes. Don't use any product with glycerin, which can create an environment conducive to yeast infections, and don't use petroleum-based lubricants.

Second, keep your pelvic floor toned. "The pelvic floor is really important in keeping your internal organs in place, preventing incontinence, and enhancing sexual pleasure," says Maureen Ryan, nurse practitioner and sex therapist.

Plus, knowing how to relax your pelvic floor muscles is helpful if you're experiencing the involuntary spasms of vaginismus.

Kegel exercises, in which you flex and relax the muscles around your vagina, will tone the pelvic floor. Or, you can purchase exercise tools to help you tone your pelvic floor muscles. This is a great way to make sure you're exercising the right muscles.

Third, use dilators if your vaginal capacity is compromised. Dilators are cylinders that come in sets with various sizes. They're meant to gradually increase the size and capacity of the vaginal opening, which can be important, especially after some cancer surgeries and treatments that constrict the vaginal opening or create scars and adhesions.

To some extent, dilators are helpful just to reassure you that you can tolerate something in your vagina again.

Start with the smallest size dilator, lubricate it, and gently insert it as far in as you can tolerate. Try doing kegel exercises, tensing and relaxing your pelvic floor muscles. Can you feel your muscles close around the dilator? Keep it in for maybe ten minutes and repeat this exercise several times a week. Move on to the next largest size when you can tolerate it.

Fourth, use a vibrator (lubricated, of course). Self-stimulation increases blood flow to your genitals and helps reacquaint you with the feelings and sensations of your body. The more stimulation you can bring to the area, the healthier it will be.

The point is to keep the vulvo-vaginal area moist and flexible, to increase blood flow, to stay responsive, to maintain capacity, so that when you and your honey are ready to start your engines, you'll both enjoy a smooth ride.

MISSING ORGASM: IS IT ME OR MY SSRI?

Are the medications you're on behind your loss of interest in sex? Are they making it more difficult for you to reach orgasm? These are tough questions. On one hand, the answer is almost always "yes": So many of the medications we take–including pain meds and sleeping aids–list lower libido as a potential side effect. On the other hand, the answer is also usually "no": In my experience, the meds aren't usually the primary cause.

With one exception. If a patient reports a notable change in her ability to reach orgasm and is taking medication for depression or anxiety, I ask if she's on an SSRI.

The most commonly used antidepressants today, SSRIs–selective serotonin reuptake inhibitors (I know it's a tongue twister)–are very effective in treating depression and anxiety disorders. Unfortunately, they also tend to dampen a woman's ability to experience orgasm.

SSRIs–some of the most commonly prescribed are Prozac (fluoxetine), Paxil (paroxetine), and Zoloft (sertraline)–work by raising levels of serotonin in the brain, enhancing neurotransmission and improving mood. The "selective" part of the name is because SSRIs affect only one type of neurotransmitter–serotonin. But higher serotonin can lead to lower libido–and missing orgasms.

Of course, depression and anxiety all by themselves often lead to reduced interest in sex, so it can be hard to tease out cause and effect. But when a patient tells me she has lost desire or orgasmic function since beginning antidepressants, I often suggest that she consider switching medications.

Other types of antidepressants, like Wellbutrin (buproprion), act on dopamine neurotransmitters and typically have fewer adverse sexual side effects. In fact, studies suggest that increased levels of dopamine in the brain may actually facilitate sexual functions including libido and orgasm.

Sometimes bupropion is prescribed in addition to an SSRI, sometimes as a replacement. Doctors can often try different combinations and dosages until they find the prescription that treats the depression without robbing patients of their orgasms.

If switching isn't an option or if changing the prescription doesn't do the trick, there are other options. Even on SSRIs, a sluggish libido or elusive orgasm will respond to increased lubrication and stimulation.

Dealing with depression is hard. We don't have to make it harder by accepting the loss of an important part of ourselves.

Chapter Seven: Health Realities and Hope

PROSTATE CANCER'S IMPACT ON YOU

Many women at this stage of life, as well as facing some changes of their own, are dealing with the very tough challenges that come when a husband has prostate cancer. Maybe you're one of them or know someone who is. Although prostate cancer is very treatable today, it's still terribly scary.

And if that weren't difficult enough, along with it may come some major issues regarding a man's sexual performance, adding even more stress and worry to the situation. Some possible side effects of surgery and/or other prostate treatments include challenges to:

» The ability to get an erection (erectile dysfunction)

» The desire to have sex

» The ability to ejaculate and have an orgasm

This affects men not only physically, but emotionally, too, since men's feelings of masculinity are often tied to their sexual performance.

And as you probably know, men are not always good at talking about sensitive subjects like this. So they often don't delve too deeply into these side effects, even with their doctors. Or they may be so distraught about the cancer itself, that it just doesn't seem important at the time.

But it is important. And that's where you can help. Communicating about it is the first step to dealing with prostate cancer and its impact on your lives. In fact, prostate cancer is often called the "couples disease" because of its broad-reaching effects in the bedroom—and elsewhere.

So while these side effects may be extremely difficult for your partner to deal with, they obviously affect you, too, especially if you have had an active and satisfying sex life. It can be a devastating loss to you both.

That's why it's critical to discuss it. Once you've begun living with this type of cancer, you need to acknowledge its impact on your relationship. It might also be a good idea to find and join a support group so you can talk with other couples about how they are dealing with this issue. I'm a big believer in sharing ideas!

The good news is, there are lots of ways to maintain sexual intimacy after prostate cancer. So instead of looking at it as the end of your sex life, look at it as a new beginning. I recommend three steps to get you started: educate, explore, and experiment.

First, *educate* yourselves about the range of solutions available that might help with the physical limitations you're now living with, including drugs such as Cialis, Viagra, and Levitra. Penile implants also have a good success rate. While that procedure may be expensive, insurance will often cover some of the costs. Penile injections are also worth considering.

There's a lot of information online about these solutions, and several books, too, such as *Saving Your Sex Life: A Guide for Men with Prostate Cancer*, by Dr. John Mulhall. Your spouse's urologist should be able to help, too. Set aside some time just to investigate what's out there and what might work for you.

You might also want to consider going to a sex therapist, who can help you in your next phase: *exploration*. If the above solutions don't appeal to you, or don't work for one reason or another, start exploring other ways to satisfy your sexual appetites given your new limitations. A sex therapist is trained to offer guidance and may have suggestions you hadn't thought of. Even if you do decide to try some of the above solutions, a sex therapist can be a tremendous help and a valuable resource. (Visit the American Association of Sex Educators, Counselors, and Therapists website for references.)

As for experimenting, if you've never tried a vibrator, this might be the time to start. And yes, your partner can be part of the enjoyment. In fact, there's a wonderful column about this by journalist Michael Castleman, who has written about sexuality for 36 years. He wrote a post called, "Gentlemen, Let's Welcome Vibrators Into Partner Sex," in which he says, "vibrators are as natural as music or candle light..." as he encourages men to experiment with their partners' favorite sex aids.

Of course, oral sex is another option, as is mutual hand stimulation. Again, this is the time to experiment and look for alternative ways that are satisfying when penetrative sex is no longer possible. It can actually be very freeing and exciting to experiment. In fact, some couples find they become even closer after they can no longer have "normal" sex.

Remember, too, that cuddling, caressing, and kissing all go a long way to maintaining intimacy. The important thing is to work together to find solutions and not let these physical constraints negatively affect your emotional connection.

QUESTIONS... AND ANSWERS

Q: How might diabetes affect my vaginal dryness treatment options?

There really are no special considerations specific to your diabetes. While I can't confidently diagnose the cause of your pain with intercourse, I can't think of a diagnosis or treatment option that would be eliminated because of your diabetes.

If you or your physician are considering systemic estrogen/progesterone, cardiovascular disease risks are taken into consideration. On the other hand, if localized (vaginal) estrogen could be part of the solution, cardiovascular disease risks are really not pertinent: The estrogen isn't absorbed systemically to any significant extent. (Don't interpret this to mean diabetics shouldn't be on hormone therapy. Many of our new studies suggest that starting hormone therapy at a younger age–closer to menopause–may actually be cardio-protective.)

I'm so glad you're taking the initiative to investigate your health and your options!

Q: What can help me experience orgasm in spite of my MS?

Whenever there are neurologic implications to a disease process, sexual response can be affected; these are difficult issues.

I did see an MS patient just recently who had not experienced orgasm in about five years. Some of the medications that treat her MS also interfered with orgasm. Fortunately, she was able to find success with a stronger vibrator for added stimulation–even though other vibrators hadn't worked for her.

Vibrators designed to have strong vibration and stimulation are better for older women and those who may have medical conditions like yours, diabetes, or medication side effects.

Q: Can I have comfortable intercourse after a vaginectomy?

A vaginectomy–surgical removal of part or all of the vagina–is most often done as part of cancer treatment. It's rarely a doctor's first choice, and some reconstruction is usually involved. Your health care provider's evaluation is an important first step.

If your health care provider believes there's physical capacity for intercourse without further reconstruction, there's more you can do to be sure that you're comfortable. A regular routine with a vaginal moisturizer will help keep your vaginal tissues healthy and elastic. You may want to use a lubricant with penetration. Make sure that you're giving yourself time (and attention!) to become fully aroused. Especially if you're having sex again after some time alone, you may be in a rush!

If you're still not comfortable, vaginal dilators may help. They can increase both the vaginal opening and the depth by gradually and gently stretching the tissue.

Keep working at it! Regaining your sex life is definitely worth some time and experimenting.

Q: How do I treat dryness and vulvodynia while taking Tamoxifen?

The most important thing is usually to re-estrogenize the vagina—with localized, not systemic estrogen. I haven't seen a single oncologist not agree to allow breast cancer patients to use this. There are a couple of really low-dose estrogen products to use in the vagina; the estrogen is not absorbed outside of that area. Vulvodynia occasionally benefits from the localized estrogen too, or there are some topical options.

A thorough and detailed pelvic exam could help to determine where the pain is arising (vulva, introitus, vagina, pelvic floor muscles, and/or vaginal cuff). Each of these has a different solution, or maybe a combination of options.

A lubricant will help somewhat with sex, but a moisturizer is more important for prevention and long-term preservation (vaginal estrogen can accomplish this, too). Some of my patients use a topical anesthetic in the area. If you have lost some caliber of the vagina—some narrowing, dilators can help restore that. Some women with longstanding pain with intercourse develop vaginismus, in which the involuntary muscles of the vagina go into spasm.

Don't stop trying! Usually we can restore comfort!

CHAPTER EIGHT

COMPONENTS OF GREAT SEX

While writing about intimacy, we came across a study seeking to understand what people consider to be Great Sex. That is, when we talk about Great Sex, what are we talking about?

In the study, authors Peggy J. Kleinplatz, A. Dana Menard, Marie-Pierre Paquet, Nicolas Paradis, Meghan Campbell, Dino Zuccarino, and Lisa Mehak, interviewed 44 people who self-identified as people who have Great Sex, and 20 sex therapists, folks who help guide people toward at least adequate sex. The resulting paper is entitled "The Components of Optimal Sexuality: A Portrait of 'Great Sex,'" and was published in 2009 in *The Canadian Journal of Human Sexuality*.

There are eight components of Great Sex the researchers identified:

» Being present.

» Connection

» Deep sexual and erotic intimacy

» Extraordinary communication

» Exploration, risk-taking

» Authenticity

» Vulnerability

» Transcendence

We thought each of these components was worthy of its own exploration.

BEING THERE

It didn't surprise me at all in reading this study that the number-one component, the one that was brought up most frequently by both experts and "practitioners," was "being present."

We're not talking, of course, about being literally, physically present (although that's fairly essential), but about being mentally and emotionally there in your body, in the moment. Here's how one woman who was interviewed for the study put it:

"The difference is when I can really just let go and completely focus and be in the moment and not have that, you know, running commentary going through my head about anything else."

For women our age, that running commentary is likely to include not only the long to-do lists of our everyday lives (what am I going to fix for dinner? how can I convince Mom that she really does need that hearing aid? I hope Sally's midterms aren't stressing her out too much), but the new and nagging concerns that come with middle-age sex (does my face look more wrinkly when I'm on top? is he going to be able to keep his erection this time? I've really got to get back into a regular routine at the gym).

There's plenty of evidence that the practice of mindfulness — non-judgmental, present-moment awareness — helps people manage things like stress and depression. It only makes sense that intensely focused attention, the ability to be fully aware of sensations experienced moment by moment, would be a central feature of sex at its best.

If you feel sometimes that you are not totally "there" during sex, that you're distracted or just going through the motions, consider learning more about meditation and mindfulness. Being more present in all aspects of your life will help you more fully experience the pleasures and sensations your body is designed to feel.

CONNECTION

We've talked about how crucial mindfulness–being mentally and emotionally present in the moment–is to enjoying great sex, sex that is "better than good." I like to think of "connection," the study's second ingredient of optimal sex, as "mindfulness times two." Connection is what happens when both partners are present together: in bed, in the moment, in each other. As one study participant describes it: "Inside my body I'm the other person's body and we're just all one together at that moment."

This sense of merging, of "two becoming one," was regularly cited as part of the experience of great sex, which has to involve "at least one moment," as one woman said, "where I can't tell where I stop and they start."

I believe that this kind of intense sexual alignment is something that becomes more accessible to us as we get older. Part of our maturity is greater acceptance of self and others, which leaves us more open to making a deep physical and spiritual connection with another person. To experience the joy of merging, of temporarily letting go of the sense of any boundary between the self and the other, a person has to know herself well–and feel safe and respected by her partner.

Which brings me to two great impediments to sexual connection: unsafe relationships and sexual trauma. If you have reasons for not feeling completely safe with a particular partner, or if you have a history that leads you to feel unsafe whenever you are in a sexual situation, you'll need to address these issues before you can experience intense connections in intimate relationships. There are resources that can help; see the last pages of this book.

But for two self-aware people who respect and desire each other and who are capable of being completely present with each other in the moment, a deeply satisfying sexual connection can happen even without penetration or orgasm. The study's authors report that great sex is often more about the level of energy between partners than about the actual physical act itself. (Check out our website's alternatives to intercourse for imaginative techniques for increasing sexual energy and connection.)

DEEP SEXUAL AND EROTIC INTIMACY

What's the difference between "connection" and intimacy? That stumped me for a bit.

Then I read this quote from one of the study's participants, describing a type of intimacy that goes beyond intense connection in the moment: "It's part of the way you act with each other long before you're actually engaged in any kind of, you know, technical sex."

I like that. I think that "the way you act with each other" before, after, and during "technical sex" is essential to deep erotic and emotional intimacy. Trust, respect, and real admiration and acceptance build the foundation for a truly intimate relationship. These are things that take time, that come with knowing each other in a profound way.

And, in my experience, you can tell if a couple has this kind of intimacy just by observing the way they interact at the grocery store or a dinner party. Do they laugh at each other's jokes? Do they exchange quick touches and knowing glances? Do they refrain from criticizing each others' tastes in breakfast cereal?

According to study participants, a deep sense of caring for one's partner is a key characteristic of sexual intimacy. One woman mentioned that her need to feel solicitude and concern had become more important to her with age: "I don't know that I'm capable of having great sex anymore without really caring about a partner."

The study's authors noted that "almost every participant identified a deep and penetrating sense of trust as characteristic of the intimacy that was part of great sex for them." They needed to trust that their partners cared for them and that the relationship was secure.

This kind of trust and intimacy doesn't just happen. It takes time and openness and communication. Especially at midlife, when our bodies and needs are changing, it's important for partners to talk with each other, to stay up-to-date on feelings and desires. Honest and caring talk about sex can be erotic in itself, and can go a long way toward creating and maintaining the deep intimacy that makes for sex that is "better than good."

EXTRAORDINARY COMMUNICATION

When they listed "communication" as an essential component of "optimal sexuality," participants in this study were talking about a lot more than talking.

Their descriptions of "extraordinary communication" often suggest a state of "heightened empathy" in which partners share themselves with each other completely, using touch and other senses as well as words. Nonverbal communication, the ability to convey and understand feelings and desires purely through physical contact, was considered essential — before, during, and after a sexual encounter.

In fact, the kind of communication the study participants refer to seems to have little connection to the conversations about sex that therapists and doctors like me recommend to couples experiencing problems with their sexual relationships. That kind of talk — I like when you touch me here, how does it feel when I do this, would you like to try something new? — may be important, even necessary, to achieve the "extraordinary communication" that makes for great sex. But the actual experience of it takes place in the moment, in the acute and continual awareness of how partner and self interact and respond.

As one study participant puts it, extraordinary communication is the ability to recognize "even if you're not told, that one kind of touch elicits a certain response in your partner and another does not."

It occurs to me that this deep empathy is what my patients are expecting, looking for, hoping for when they protest that talking about sex diminishes or even ruins the act itself. We all wish our partners could know exactly what we want and how we feel without being told.

But in my experience, this kind of extraordinary communication doesn't happen unless couples first invest time and effort in a lot of pretty ordinary communication — honest and explicit talk about sex and feelings and desires.

EXPLORATION AND FUN

One of the qualities we haven't yet discussed is the willingness to experiment with your partner. Respondents referred to great sex as an "adventure" and a "discovery process" in which they learned new things about themselves and their partners. In the study, however, this quality was often described in a playful, lighthearted context.

Anything we do repeatedly for a long time tends to become routine. We trot along the same worn dog path in which every bump and bend is familiar. After a while, any routine activity, sex included, can become a bore and then maybe a chore. That's why here at MiddlesexMD, we often prescribe a healthy dose of novelty to spice up the routine—a change of position, place, or props, especially for partners who have been together for a long time.

But great sex goes beyond trying new toys. These respondents seemed to revel in the joyful aspect of experimentation, of trying new things together. Exploring new dimensions of sex wasn't a test they passed or failed; it wasn't medicine they took because it was good for them; it didn't involve one partner trying to "sell" the other on something new. The outcome didn't matter; how they looked didn't matter. What mattered was that both partners were engaged in the adventure and were having a good time doing it. Often, too, the exploration uncovered new qualities about the relationship or themselves.

Playfulness has to be genuine, and this joyful experimentation probably also requires another aspect of great sex that the researchers identified: extraordinary communication. But whatever the quality of our communication or spirit of adventure, it's always possible—and helpful—to be open to new things, to be willing to relinquish the safety of routine and even boredom, and to step into new territory, even if it involves some risk and some energy. And if playing together also contributes to a great sex life, well then, game on.

AUTHENTICITY

Just be yourself, our mothers told us when we worried about what to wear and say and do on our first date with that special someone. Such hard advice to follow when we wanted to be cool and sexy and in control — everything, in other words, that our real selves were not.

Mom was clearly onto something. Participants in this study listed "being completely and genuinely oneself" as an essential component of great sex.

People who were interviewed for the study described feeling completely uninhibited and unselfconscious with their sexual partners, able to reveal themselves physically, emotionally, and spiritually without fear or shame. One woman spoke about the exquisite joy she experienced when she exposed her "real self" to her husband in bed. "It was just so shocking to me that I could actually express these things and, he was right there loving it and doing it with me."

This is really the definition of intimacy, isn't it — sharing your real, genuine, authentic self with another person?

Unfortunately, experts tell us, the ability to just be yourself doesn't get easier as we get older. Over time we become even more practiced at hiding our uncool, unsexy, and out-of-control selves behind social and cultural masks.

According to the study, people who have experienced the emotional power of authentic intimacy — of being genuinely seen and known by another person — often say that getting there required them to first understand and reject the "rules" about what is or isn't sexy, desirable, and possible between two people who love each other. Moving beyond existing scripts to try out new sexual roles and techniques actually helped liberate them to be true to their "real" selves.

VULNERABILITY

Scary, huh?

Being completely vulnerable to another human being can be scary, even if that person is our life partner. Yet, just as sex involves physical nudity, great sex demands a similar level of psychological nakedness.

Study participants described this level of vulnerability as "being able to put your entire being in someone else's hands" or "like jumping off a cliff" and yet feeling safe. It's a deliberate act of surrender to your partner with nothing held back. And for the respondents of this study, vulnerability made the difference between good sex and great sex.

Vulnerability cuts to the heart of self-preservation. Our instinct is to protect ourselves, to hide just a little, not to completely bare our throats. We may do this because we're afraid of rejection, or of being ignored, or of being controlled, or because we've been hurt in the past, maybe even in loving relationships. We may also be dragging into our adult lives some unexamined anxieties from our childhood—fears that can exert a powerful influence no matter how outdated or irrational they may be. And the bedroom with all its intimacy and nakedness is just the place where these fears, past and present, are likely to intrude.

Acknowledging and examining what holds us back from self-surrender to a trusted and loved partner is a good and healthy exercise. After all, we've probably developed more mature ways to handle pain and rejection than when we were children. And these unpleasant emotions can also reveal to us areas in which we still need to grow. What better place to practice trust, vulnerability, and self-revelation than in the midst of a loving relationship?

So examine your barriers to intimacy. What's holding you back? What are you afraid of? What keeps you from being vulnerable? Then risk sharing those fears. That's the first important step toward deeper levels of intimacy. You might also practice asking for what you want as well as asking your partner what feels good or what you could do that would be more pleasurable.

Taking the risk of deeper self-revelation can also encourage our partners to respond in kind. But in any case, what do we have to lose? Some outdated fears? A twinge of embarrassment or pain? And we stand to gain a deeper, more satisfying relationship with the person we're closest to. And, maybe, great sex.

So, go ahead. Jump.

TRANSCENDENCE

> "There are many paths to heaven, and sex is one of them."
> –Abraham Maslow

Maslow, the humanist psychologist who invented the term "peak experience," would know exactly what participants in the "Optimal Sexuality" study mean when they say that "transformation" is an essential part of extraordinary sex.

People interviewed for the study used words like "bliss," "peace," "awe," and "ecstasy" to describe this transcendent aspect of peak sexual experiences. Some compared it to the "high" that can be achieved through meditation. Others used religious language to describe the feeling, calling it "revelatory," "eternal," "an epiphany."

"At this moment," one participant said, "we were in the presence of God."

It can seem a little over the top, I know. But while not all of us can say (like one study participant) that we've experienced sex that felt like "floating in the universe of light and stars and music and sublime peace," many of us can relate to what singer Marvin Gaye called "sexual healing." Physical and emotional intimacy can simply make us feel better, more in harmony with ourselves and our partners.

The transformative power of great sex that "can change you, can make you more than you are," goes beyond the bedroom, I think. True sexual healing carries over into our everyday lives, makes us calmer, happier, more loving people.

For some of us, hormonal changes or the special stresses of midlife have reduced the power of sexual healing and transformation in our lives. Remember, though, if we understand what's happening to our bodies, we can find ways to bring that power back.

You can find your own little piece of heaven, right here on earth.

RESOURCES

RESOLVE TO SPEAK UP!

I was struck by this sentence in a report on research with women aged 45 to 65 experiencing menopause: "As a generation, they have yet to develop a voice for this situation, and many remain silent rather than proactively seeking help."

Really? We are the generation who, in high school, bought Our Bodies, Ourselves to better understand menstruation and sex. We pushed the boundaries to study science, go to medical school, become executives, compete for construction jobs, run our own businesses. We bought Marlo Thomas's Free to Be You and Me for our kids.

But in my own experience as a physician, I see evidence that it's true. When my practice included women of all ages, patients came in ready to talk in detail about physical symptoms—and emotional effects—related to pregnancy or fertility or uncooperative or uncomfortable periods. I don't recall as many conversations about symptoms of menopause, especially as they related to sexuality.

In the last few years, since I've focused my practice on midlife women, those who come to see me are ready to talk. This may have encouraged me to think we've made more progress than we have; this "REVEAL" (Revealing Vaginal Effects at Mid-Life) study is a useful reality check.

This research found that 41 percent of postmenopausal women had not talked to anyone about their sexual health in the previous year. Just over a third had talked to a health care provider; fewer—30 percent—had spoken to their partner or significant other.

The oldest women in the study—60 to 65—were least likely to have spoken to anyone at all. The younger women—45 to 49—were more likely to have spoken to someone: health care providers, partners, and then female friends.

Why does any of this matter? Consider the other findings of this research:

» While almost all of the women surveyed were familiar with hot flashes as a symptom of menopause, fewer than half were aware that vulvar/vaginal pain was another symptom.

» A quarter of those surveyed experienced pain during sex; most of those women still have sex—in spite of the discomfort—at least once a month.

» The majority—80 percent—of the women who experienced pain during sex assumed it was a "normal part of getting older."

That's a whole lot of women who aren't aware that sex can still be pleasurable and pain-free, even after menopause. And it's a whole lot of women who won't even broach the topic with their health care providers, because they assume that nothing can be done.

So! Clearly, it's up to you! I imagine a whole lot of conversations between best women friends, women and their partners, sisters… and, for the sake of the next generation, between us and our daughters.

There are symptoms of menopause beyond hot flashes, night sweats, and mood swings. Decreasing hormone levels affect our vaginal and genital tissues, but they don't spell the end of sexuality—or comfortable intercourse. There are things any woman can do to restore or preserve her sexual health, and we need to talk about them!

HAVING "THE TALK"—WITH YOUR DOCTOR

Just when you thought you were home free—the kids are grown, and you've somehow gotten through multiple birds-and-bees talks. But now you find the shoe is on the other foot, and you're the one needing information about sex. Maybe a health issue is affecting your sex life, or maybe your body is responding differently, or maybe you're just not as responsive as you used to be. Where do you go for straight talk about these nitty-gritty topics?

According to a presentation I heard at the International Society for the Study of Women's Sexual Health (ISSWSH) conference "physicians often do not talk to their patients about sex." It occurred to me that the effect of this oversight is similar to neglecting the "talk" with our kids, i.e. you end up muddling along with misinformation, rumors, or half-truths.

Oddly, doctors cite similar reasons (excuses?) as the rest of us for avoiding the "talk" with their patients: They don't have time; they don't feel comfortable; they don't know enough about this medical subspecialty to feel competent and helpful.

To be honest, doctors do operate under very tight time constraints in the course of a normal day. Also, sometimes, after talking about health and body parts for years, we forget how uncomfortable it might be for you to bring up what you consider an embarrassing problem. Rest assured, however, that we've probably discussed that problem before with someone.

None of this lets anyone off the hook. Sex is an important component of physical and mental health and well-being, and if you have questions or problems, who better to discuss them with than your doctor? If your doctor isn't taking the initiative, here are some ways to help get the conversation started.

» Write down your questions. This exercise may help you clarify what you want to talk about, and it will definitely help you to remember everything.

» Prime the pump. At the beginning of your appointment, mention that you'd like to discuss some sexual issue that you've been experiencing. Or, get more specific—that you'd like to explore your options for vaginal lubricants or whether your medication might be diminishing your sexual interest.

» Be clear, specific, and thorough. Don't leave something out because it's too embarrassing or doesn't seem pertinent. You wouldn't neglect to mention to your mechanic the little whirring noise in the rear axle when you turn left. Why would you omit an itch or pain or change you experience in your body?

Once you get over the initial hurdle of actually saying the S-word in front of your doctor, you may find it much easier to talk about sex in the future. After all, as you told your children all those years ago, sex is just a natural part of life.

FOR MORE INFORMATION

MiddlesexMD.com has more information on all of the topics included in this book, as well as products especially selected for safe and effective use by midlife women.

MENOPAUSE CARE PROVIDERS (NAMS)
The North American Menopause Society is the professional organization of caregivers who have undergone study and training to care particularly for women in perimenopause and beyond. NAMS maintains a referral service of physicians and caregivers who belong to their organization. Clinicians with the credential of NCMP (NAMS Certified Menopause Practitioner) have demonstrated special competency in the field of menopause. Go to www.Menopause.org and click on "For Women" to find someone in your area.

OBSTETRICIAN/GYNECOLOGISTS (OB/GYN)
If you have had kids, you probably have an Ob/Gyn on your health care team already. If you haven't had kids, and you are having pain with intercourse or other difficulties with vulvo-vaginal tissues or with your pelvic organs, you may wish to ask your doctor for a referral to one of these specialists. The American Congress of Obstetricians and Gynecologists maintains a Web listing of these specialists in your area; go to www.ACOG.org and click on "For Patients."

PHYSICAL THERAPISTS
Some physical therapists specialize in vulvo-vaginal and pelvic therapies, helpful in treating a number of conditions that can inhibit your sex life as you age. Your local Ob/Gyn will know the nearest specialists in your area, or contact the American Physical Therapy Association for a referral to a therapist trained in women's health. Go to www.APTA.org and click on "For the Public."

COGNITIVE THERAPISTS
A woman's libido is affected by her psyche and by social pressures as well as by her physicality. All three of these influences change as we age. Psychological counseling can be especially helpful for couples working to reestablish closeness in their relationships. It can help a woman manage the after effects of sexual trauma. It can help in the management of chronic stress, anxiety, depression and pain, all of which can hurt our sexuality. To find a therapist near you, you might ask your family doctor, or contact the American Board of Couple and Family Psychology through their website, www.ABPP.org or by phone, (919) 537 8031.

SEX THERAPISTS
Aging can really wreak havoc with a couple's sexuality. A counselor or therapist who specializes in sexual and relationship problems can save us years of pain, miscommunication, and frustration. Sex therapists begin by helping couples understand the role of intimacy in their lives, and normal sexual functioning at any age. Therapists help people gain and share a deeper understanding of their sexual identities and beliefs, which also change as we age. Couples emerge from counseling better understanding the role of intimacy and attachment in their relationships, and how their verbal and nonverbal communication affects them. Ask your doctor for a referral, or find a nearby therapist through the American Association of Sex Educators, Counselors, and Therapists at www.AASECT.org.

STI SCREENING
As long as we're sexually active, we're vulnerable to sexually transmitted infections. That's the simple truth. While you may have gotten away with less-than-safe sex when you were younger, don't play with that fire now. The Center for Disease Control offers a resource for learning about STIs, protecting yourself and your partner, and getting tested, at hivtest.cdc.gov.

DOMESTIC ABUSE ASSISTANCE
Aging can bring changes in our sexuality that are frustrating for us and our partners. Frustration and anger can build and spiral out of control in a household, leading couples to abusive situations. If you think things have gotten out of hand for you or for someone you know and love, help is at www.theHotline.org or 1 (800) 799 SAFE (7233).